LEAD LIFT AND LEAVE A LEGACY

Shining a Light on the Remarkable Journeys of Women Leaders and Their Mentors

A COMPILATION
BY RACHEL RUBIN WILKINS

Lead, Lift, and Leave a Legacy
Shining a Light on the Remarkable Journeys of Women Leaders and Their Mentors
TW Legacy Publishing

Published by **TW Legacy Publishing**, St. Louis, MO

All contributing authors to this anthology have submitted their chapters to an editing process, and have accepted the recommendations of the editors at their own discretion. All authors have approved their chapters prior to publication.

Cover, Interior Design, and Project Management:
  Davis Creative Publishing, DavisCreativePublishing.com
Writing Coach and Editor: Jackie Duty

Compilation by Rachel Rubin Wilkins

Publisher's Cataloging-in-Publication
Names: Wilkins, Rachel Rubin, compiler.
Title: Lead, lift, and leave a legacy : shining a light on the remarkable journeys of women
      leaders and their mentors / a compilation by Rachel Rubin Wilkins.
Description: St. Louis, MO : TW Legacy Publishing, [2025]
Identifiers: ISBN: 979-8-9925195-0-1 (paperback) | 979-8-9925195-2-5 (hardback) |
      979-8-9925195-1-8 (ebook) | LCCN: 2025901685
Subjects: LCSH: Leadership in women. | Women executives. | Mentoring in business. |
      Employees-- Coaching of. | LCGFT: Self-help publications. | BISAC: SELF-HELP /
      Motivational & Inspirational. | SELF-HELP / Personal Growth / General. | BUSINESS &
      ECONOMICS / Mentoring & Coaching.
Classification: LCC: HD6054.3 .L43 2025 | DDC: 658.4092082--dc23

"In my theatrical line of work, a performer who can sing, act, and dance is called a 'triple threat.' Rachel Rubin Wilkins is the educational and entrepreneurial equivalent of a triple threat in life. She is one of those rare individuals you meet along life's journey who simultaneously loves learning, loves helping others, and loves paying it forward. She is a threat...in the most glorious way possible."

Robert Mark Morgan
Designer, Teaching Professor, & Creativity Evangelist
Author of *The Art of Scenic Design: A Practical Guide to the Creative Process*

"Rachel is a vortex of energy and positivity. She is an institution builder with a nurturing spirit and an appetite for challenge. Someone who makes the world a better place."

Dr. Ron King
Emeritus Professor – Washington University Saint Louis
Founder of Medallion Adventure Club

"'What remains is what we leave behind,' a close friend once wisely said. Mentorship, the epitome of leadership, is born of humility, dedication, challenges, and triumphs. Mentors illuminate the path, transforming the seemingly impossible into reality. They offer hope in times of darkness and unwavering support amidst setbacks.

Rachel stands as a testament to these ideals, a force to be reckoned with who proudly joins the ranks of these remarkable women whose actions have reshaped our world. This book invites you to experience their journeys firsthand, inspiring you to lead, lift, and leave a legacy."

Luke Kratky
Vice President
NGA Programs at Omni Federal

"In a world where success often depends on meaningful guidance, Rachel Rubin Wilkins curates an essential resource through this powerful anthology on mentoring. As both the co-editor and compiler of these insightful chapters, Rachel weaves together diverse voices and experiences to address the challenges women face in business. Her dedication to mentoring young women shines through, offering a roadmap that empowers them to lead, uplift others, and create lasting change. This timely and valuable collection provides practical wisdom for anyone seeking to navigate and thrive in their professional journey."

Dr. Simone M. Cummings
Dean of the George Herbert Walker School of Business & Technology
Webster University

"I've had the privilege of working with Rachel for over five years. As a mentor to hundreds in the military community, her impact on career progression is undeniable. Rachel's leadership has driven positive change, advocating tirelessly for soldiers and their families across multiple organizations. Her ability to unite diverse groups and foster collaboration has been vital to the community's success. Her insights and experiences have led, inspired, and created meaningful change for professionals pivoting into new careers."

Scott Raether
Employment Program Director; Career Readiness Consultant
United States Scott Air Force Base

"As a student beginning my career, being a part of the LeadHERship Fellows Program has aided my personal growth and career advancement by providing connections with experienced, professional women. Through personal, easy-to-read stories, this book provides valuable insights into the knowledge and advice that young adults stand to gain from mentorships."

Remi Barnett
Business Psychology College Student
Barrett Honors College; Arizona State University

"Rachel Wilkins leads with her whole being. Without fanfare, without drawing attention to herself, she just gets to work, laying foundations and building communities where deep support and mentoring opportunities naturally arise and thrive."

Dr. Lynnea Brumbaugh, PhD
Founder of The ExecutiveOS
Author of Flow, Know, and Grow

"As a first-generation college graduate, I owe my success to the mentors who invested in me and believed in my potential. Lead, Lift, and Leave a Legacy is an inspiring collection of stories from remarkable female leaders, and I'm grateful to Rachel for her "LeadHERship," bringing these voices together to empower others."

Nan Barnes
Certified Career Management Coach and Gallup-Certified Strengths Coach
Co-author of the Vault Guide to the International MBA Job Search

Dedication

*This book is dedicated to
my family, affectionately known as Team Wilkins.
"You are the STARS that bring light to my life!"*

Hunter, Kate, Ethan, Sarah, and Hanah,

*May you always be able to recognize
the stars in your constellations
and know that you SHINE within them.
I am grateful for you.
Trust and be confident in yourself, and
your light will be a beacon for others to follow,
leaving your own legacy.*

Acknowledgments

Recognizing the STARS in My Constellations

To Team Wilkins: T.E.A.M.—Together Everyone Accomplishes More!

Patrick—thank you for your constant support, understanding, and encouragement during my passion projects. I could not have done this without your perspective, upbeat attitude, advice, and guidance. After 30 years, we have a lifetime of mentorship behind us and ahead of us. Thank you for keeping me focused on my "why" when circumstances became challenging and for your patience as we moved through this process to arrive at this meaningful mission. Love you!

Hunter, Kate, Ethan, Hanah, and Sarah—I appreciate your time, advice, love, and patience as this bucket list endeavor unfolded before your eyes, watching me balance all the roles. I appreciate your feedback, positivity, and faith that we could do this together with grace and gratitude. Keep shining your light to the world, this book is dedicated to you!

To the co-authors:

For the remarkable co-authors who joined us for a myriad of reasons. Thank you for the courage to step out of your comfort zone and shine your light! Each one of you has a special gift and light within. I am honored to know you. While shining your light, you shine on a path for others to follow and emulate your career and personal successes. I am excited to hear how your mentors and families receive your chapter and how you will bring love and joy to the world for each reader.

To the LeadHERship Fellows:

Thank you for staying engaged in this project from four different universities in three different states. Your reverse mentorship, dedication to the survey, and desire to show up in our monthly Zoom meetings were important. Your voice mattered as we provided skills, guidance, and advice for our next generation of LeadHERs – YOU!

To my "Board of Advisors":

- Marianne Biangardi
- Maxine Clark
- Simone Cummings
- Denise Huber
- Dr. Ron King
- Luke Kratky
- Mitch Meyers
- Rob Morgan
- Jaime Nunnelee
- Scott Raether

Your unwavering support and boost of confidence gave me the shot in the arm to stay tenacious and relentlessly confident in this project and in life. I am grateful for you!

To the Davis Creative Publishing team:

Cathy, Julie, Jackie, and team, your process, knowledge, reassurance, and direction kept us on track to produce incredible results for our co-authors and for readers worldwide who will be touched by this book in their hands. Thank you for respecting and cherishing the importance of this mentoring mission to make our world a better place.

To my extended family and friends:

Thank you for your support over the years. The ripple effect of encouragement from family and friends cascades down into each member of our family and to each level of friendship, echoing hope and a promise of faith for tomorrow.

Mom, Dad, Liz, and Marty, I am grateful we have each other to remember the good times and support each other through the challenging times.

To the women I interviewed:

I am grateful for the more than 136 women I met with to discuss the mission of mentorship. Unanimously, everyone stated that mentoring and authentic relationships mattered. Your powerful conversations kept me moving forward, enhanced my net worth by adding you to my network, and allowed me to hear your stories and struggles (at times, with tissues) to create a powerful mission. Whether or not your journey led you to write this time, your stories were heard. I loved getting texts after our conversations as you reached out to mentors and thanked them, even if you did not join this anthology. Keep paying it forward.

To the reader:

The goal of this anthology, the secret weapon against depression, relies on the hope that we promote through gratitude and honoring those people who support us in life. From gratitude, we evoke happiness; from happiness, we promote joy. With gratitude, happiness, and joy, depression is diminished, and the feeling of being alone is replaced with hope, community, significance, and success.

TABLE OF CONTENTS

FOREWORD

I am a child of privilege. Not the privilege most people think of but the privilege of growing up in America in the 1950s when growth and expansion were everywhere. My parents were first-generation Americans from Albany, New York. They were high school-educated and hard-working. My father learned his trade in the military—to be an electrician. My mother got her first job as a member of the typing pool right out of high school at 14 years old working for the Governor's wife—Eleanor Roosevelt. Eleanor loved her spunk and her type and shorthand skills and brought Mom to DC to be her traveling secretary when Franklin became President.

Post World War II, my parents "immigrated" to Miami, Florida, where the weather was grand, and opportunity was everywhere. Construction was booming and electricians were needed. His military service entitled him to access the GI Bill home mortgage loan, and my parents were able to buy a home in Coral Gables, Florida. Our community was new and strong. I always felt safe and that I could depend on my neighbors. These neighbors were the beginning of my network of people, friends, and mentors in my community at a young age. Friends, teachers, and local businesses encouraged me to believe in myself and always be curious. I never felt small. Local leaders and role models played a role in who I am today, shaping my self-confidence. These relationships taught me many lessons.

Like many young women, we admired our mothers. My mother, Annie, was a red-headed 4'9" firebrand. Having Eleanor Roosevelt as her boss and mentor, she learned to think big and to bring a broad perspective of people to the table—Black, White, male, female, tall, short, native-born, or foreign. You name it—they were all welcome at my mother's table to create change. Luckily, she invited me to her table, and I saw firsthand what passion and hard work can do.

During World War II, as she traveled the country with the First Lady, she saw the inequities of children in asylums all over the country, and her passion to serve children arose from this experience. After Franklin D. Roosevelt died, Eleanor gave her employees a small bit of money to return home with and create a solution for one of the problems they saw in their travels across America. My mother and her friends founded a school for children with Down syndrome in Miami. Life for children with disabilities began to change as women across America found the power to make change whether it was fighting for a cure for polio or the need for seat belts or to stand up against drunk driving. They urged the US Government to create a Department of Education and provide quality education for our children.

My mother's work ethic, determination, and compassion for others left an impact on me, which influenced my drive, love for education and children, and curiosity to solve problems. She taught me the true math that matters: 1+1 must equal 100 to be a force necessary to make a difference! She was a great mom, wife, and community contributor. Her example reminded me that service is important and to give back to your community.

Graduating from high school in 1967, I wanted to change the world. I loved history and politics, and I wanted to be able to be a person of influence. While I admired my mother's passion for non-profit work, my curiosity led me down a different path. Her example gave me confidence to lead in business and succeed in my career throughout my life. As a retail enthusiast, my passion to create tangible products and retail experiences for families found at Build-A-Bear spearheaded these lovable bears to land in many communities in the world, bringing "a little more heart to life." These unique opportunities focus on quality experiences that build relationships and make lasting memories, one teddy bear at a time. Build-A-Bear products bring joy to others and reach people in ways I had never imagined. These lessons have been the foundation that continues to support what I build today.

My most recent post-retirement endeavor, the creation of the Delmar DivINe, serves the non-profit space. The reimagination of a historic but abandoned hospital has had a huge impact on the 30+ nonprofits we house, the 150 affordable apartments, and an entire neighborhood is on the rise. The concept supports thousands of people finding their passion and purpose in the world. The Delmar DivINe community provides a place for like minds to mentor, explore, share, and guide each other through the everyday lessons in business development, collaboration, and success. My mother would be so proud that I finally became a social activist, a collaborator at an entirely different impact level!

After years of networking, mentoring, and building relationships in communities all over the world, Rachel has created a space for our community to connect, learn, grow, and empower each other as we seek out our passions in life. Her workshop, Recognize the Stars in Your Constellations, teaches us the importance of recognizing others and showing gratitude when people support each other. Her LeadHERship movement has gathered women who are sharing their career journey with tales of networking, mentorship, and relationship building that expand their stars and constellations as they Lead, Lift, and Leave a Legacy. In this collection, authors share stories that cast a light on career opportunities and pivots, creating hope in the world as people make career moves that align with their passion. This light shines as an example, empowering women to move forward past obstacles.

Mentoring is a two-way street. You have to be open to coaching, to observing, to listening, and to learning. These relationships create a multiplier effect that has an impact and reaches farther than the eye can see. Be a coach, mentor, advisor, and lead others to overcome. As I have shared previously my power math now requires us to think, 1+1+1 = 1,000 and multiplies the power of connection. Relationships are key to empowering others and mentoring our community to build a better tomorrow. As there are no easy solutions to today's challenges, we are less alone when we act together and collaborate: starting within our own neighborhoods.

Happy networking,
Maxine Clark
CEO, Clark-Fox Family Foundation
Founder, Build-A-Bear Workshop
Chief INspirator, The Delmar DivINe

Mentoring Boards: Build-A-Bear Workshop, Footlocker Inc, Big Dot of Happiness, PBS, New American Foundation

Anne, Maxine Clark's mother in the white blazer,
was Eleanor Roosevelt's private traveling secretary during World War II.

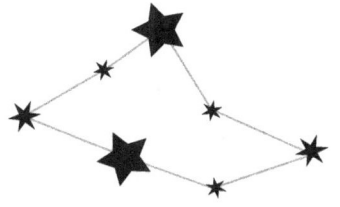

LeadTHEM:
The Mission of Mentoring

"Nothing can dim the light that shines within"
—Maya Angelou

The Mission of Mentoring has set the trajectory and shaped the path of my future. In the summer of 2023, I received a Social Cognitive Career Theory (SCCT) Certificate on the topic of mentoring from the National Science Foundation. The class was taught by Professor Robert Morgan from Washington University in Saint Louis (supported by Professor Anita Balaraman from University of California—Berkeley), who has a passion to teach about mentoring and its connections to career advancement. The Social Cognitive Theory, originally developed by Albert Bandura, connects the dots between learned behaviors, and the dynamic relationship between environmental influences, personal factors, and behaviors. This psychological theory depicts the effects of the cognitive processes (motivation, concepts, and judgment) as influencers on an individual's behaviors and environmental factors. A tenet of this theory is that personal self-efficacy, expected outcomes, goal setting, and self-evaluation have an effect on individual successes and accomplishments. These topics and their delivery were exceptionally interesting, and I yearned to learn more about this exploration of the social sciences and their impact on career pathways.

My oldest daughter and I applied for admission to the class together, and we made the cut! On the first day of class, my daughter kindly shared with the virtual class that her "mother was her role model and person she looked up to" in one of the opening icebreakers. Shocked and delighted, I was reminded of the critical impact we make daily, not only in our professional lives but in our personal lives as well. This impact shows up in the most interesting and important places through observational learning.

I knew role modeling and mentorship mattered. Engaged in mentoring, coaching, and advising for over 30 years, these roles took on various shapes along my non-linear life path. When the class ended, I wanted to learn more. I reached out to Professor Robert Morgan and asked, "What's next? How can I help further this mission and spread the word on social media?" He replied, "Your timing comes at a prescient time as I am unable to run the fall session. Would you like to take on that role? We thought that you might be the perfect fit for that role for fall. Let us know if you are interested."

Once again, shocked and delighted, I said "yes" with little debate. He replied, "Thrilled you're taking the reins!" Just like that, an adjunct professor was born. I was empowered to accomplish a goal from my Milestone Manifesto, also known as my Aspirational Bucket List.

The professor role was wildly different than being a student in the class. It required sharpening old teaching skills and learning from alternative angles. As I prepared, practiced, and received mentorship from my previous professors, I experienced the social and cognitive art of mentoring from a new dimension. I exercised attentive listening, strategic lesson planning, learning from mistakes, being curious, trying new things, recognizing strengths and weaknesses, and celebrating student successes, all the while under the umbrella of mentoring. Intrigued, I delved into research on my own and found my passion and purpose.

In my research, I discovered an article from *Gallup News*, May 17, 2023, which headlined

"U.S. Depression Rates Reach New Highs," by Dan Witters. U.S. adults who report having been diagnosed with depression at some point in their lifetime reached 29.0%, nearly 10 percentage points higher than in 2015. This was a significant climb. The percentage of Americans that have or are being treated for depression increased, to 17.8%, up about seven points over the same period. "The most recent results, obtained Feb. 21-28, 2023, are based on 5,167 U.S. adults surveyed by the internet as part of the Gallup Poll, a probability-based panel of about 100,000 adults across all 50 states and the District of Columbia."

Compared to the 2017 results, the fastest rising rates impact these groups: women, young adults, and Black and Hispanic adults. For women, this rate has risen twice as fast as men since 2017. Primarily impacting women between the ages of 18 to 29 and 30 to 44, having the greatest rise in depression rates compared to women over 44 years of age. Men in these age groups have increased depression rates as well, just not as high as the rate of their female counterparts. For our young adults, there are more reports on loneliness during and after the global pandemic. This group requires more social interactions than older adults. Feelings of anger, worry, and sadness also contribute to signs of depression and hit harder for lower-income households and those just starting their careers. Americans are not alone. Depression has also hit globally, with estimates suggesting a rate of 19% of the people (America reported at 22%) having experienced depression or anxiety in other countries.

Reflecting on my own journey in my twenties, I wanted to do something for our *next* generation: for my children, your children, and their children. What do we do? Start a mentoring mission: LeadTHEM. How? Enter the LeadTHEM Project. Through mentorship, creating communities, and combating loneliness, we can start to make a difference, one relationship at a time. The LeadTHEM Project is not gender specific and involves both men and women. Since women are the hardest hit, with the greatest rise in depression, and the fact that I could recognize this in my community in numerous local organizations I work within, out emerged the LeadHERship Mission: *Lead, Lift, and Leave a Legacy.* This anthology of authentically empowering mentoring stories from women shining a light on their personal and professional lives will bridge the gap between loneliness or despair to stories of empowerment, community, confidence, success, and achievement. These stories reflect historical resiliency, intention, and devotion from women in their twenties to eighties and every decade in between. This bouquet of positive, uplifting stories will not only fashion a way forward but also give tangible advice and takeaways to support women and men, bringing power to the impact we each can make as we mentor, advise, coach, and extend our light to others.

For role models to emerge, they need to be seen. As a small action to solve part of this problem, I created an internship program in 2023 and had seven interns for my consulting company, Team of Seven Consulting, LLC. The group was a coed group united to learn more about digital marketing, event project management, public speaking, and customer service. The following summer, four interns and one senior fellow returned for the LeadHERship Fellows program. This fellowship included the Recognize the Stars in Your Constellations Workshop, fundraising for non-profits, mentoring, LinkedIn coaching, research, and publishing opportunities. These LeadHERs are all contributors to the book as co-authors, marketers, and/or research assistants (see their LeadHERship Fellows section in this book).

In the SCCT certification class, I taught current students and Washington University alums from around the country and in Europe. I decided to ask the alumni to be Spotlight Mentors and shed a light on their careers, referring to topics and definitions we were covering in class. It was at this intersection of sharing and shedding a light through the "STAR" speakers that I realized deeper learning and connections started to happen. Inquisitive conversations emerged to solve burning questions and encourage growth and development. As the Spotlight Mentors shared their stories, they provided testimonials, tips, and advice—and simultaneously, unknowingly, mentoring at large. As the adjunct professor sharing my journey, I am one woman. I have an interesting, non-linear path in recruitment, education, marketing, and event strategy, 20 years as an Army military spouse, and 27 years as CEO of Team Wilkins, one of the most rewarding roles of all. Spotlight Mentors gave the opportunity for more voices to be heard and a variety of career paths to be illuminated.

Currently, there are countless career fields. By 2035, many jobs will become obsolete or trend to fill roles in technology, AI, MI (machine intelligence), geospatial, cybersecurity, sustainability, healthcare, digital arts, education, or space exploration. There are career fields we have yet to think about that will emerge, and our world will continue to change and adapt. Research shows, to prevent a huge gap in our workforce development, career mentors will be needed.

In fact, the need for mentorship is now. In this mission of mentorship, more women need to share their extraordinary, everyday stories to expose career path decisions, demonstrate how to pivot, or advance in various careers while building strong families and maintaining rich personal lives. This is why I invited and championed the extraordinary women in this anthology to illuminate their diverse personal and professional paths. How do we do it all as women? One day, one step at a time, and never giving up. We do this by uniting, arm in arm, leading with confidence, grace, and gratitude. Lifting each other up while extending our light within ourselves to *shine* and to *Lead, Lift, and Leave a Legacy.*

Rachel Rubin Wilkins
TW Legacy Publishing
Team of Seven Consulting, LLC

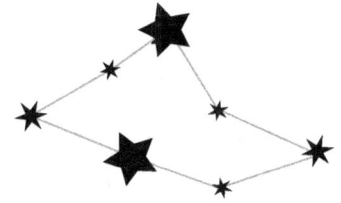

Rachel Rubin Wilkins

Run Your Race

"Let us run with perseverance the race that is set before us."
—Hebrews 12:1

"GO, you've got this…you're hitting your splits! You will make it to the state championship." Although this motivational voice spoke from decades ago, I can still hear the empowering words of my high school track coach. His positive passion propelled our track team to greatness, practice after practice, to victories at meets, districts, sectionals, and then on to the state championship. His style of leadership not only served our team well in high school but for decades to come, as many of us continue to run today. Our resolute spirit, fueled by motivation, determination, discipline, and clear goal setting, were areas that served us throughout life. He kept us accountable and pushed us physically and mentally to become the best version of ourselves.

There are times when we do not realize the ripple effect we make just by showing up, doing our best, and extending our passion and motivation to others. I did not tell my coach until almost thirty years later about the impact he made on my life during high school. "Rachel Rubin!" Coach exclaimed with excitement and a tone I recognized as he entered the room. I was thrust back in time to a place I had not been to in years. A youthful sense of purpose and accomplishment rushed through me as my mind circled back to training sessions, time charts, intervals, drills, and goals reached. I had an instant eagerness to tell him about the significant impact he made on me that changed my life and extended into my family. He was the first person to introduce me to Scripture, enhancing my faith. He pushed our team to greatness, to overcome obstacles, to be courageous, and to believe in ourselves while also cherishing the individual. He cared, he advised, he coached, and he guided us. His impact not only influenced me then but had a ripple effect on my future self.

I continued to run past high school, competing in several races: The Missouri Show-Me-State Games and three Army Ten Milers sprinkled in with a few half marathons, a few small five-kilometer races, and running the Marine Corp Marathon with my husband – a mutual bucket list item. As an Army wife raising five children while my husband was often deployed, running was my sanity, my personal space, my stress relief, and a very healthy addiction. I passed this love for accomplishment and self-fulfillment to my children. They, too, have registered for their own races and feel the benefits of accomplishing and achieving these personal goals, all five having run several races themselves. During a deployment, the children and I trained for one of our favorite family races, the Plains Peanut Festival: Plains, Peanuts, and a President. After each of us placed in our races, we were awarded the "Plains Road Race Family" by former President Jimmy Carter and received individual trophies from him. These events inspired our children, who were between five and eleven years old at the time, to keep running into their twenties. These moments are times we will never forget as a military family. Thank you, Coach, for creating a sustaining, positive running environment that sparked a flame in me and my legacy.

Impact of mentors

"One of the greatest values of mentors is the ability to see ahead what others cannot see and to help them navigate a course to their destination."
—John C. Maxwell

Many years ago, in preparation for my husband's deployment to places unknown, we traveled home to St. Louis to visit with family. While the children visited with their grandparents, my husband and I had a date night at a Build-A-Bear Workshop to create five stuffed bears for our young children. The mission was to record my husband's voice in each bear so that at nighttime (or anytime), the children could have a reminder of their daddy's voice while he was away. As a military family with a dad in the special operations community, deployments were unexpected and dangerous. I wanted meaningful mementos for each child prior to his departures. These cute, lovable toys became bedtime "tools" to make the routine more manageable while providing a needed memory of their dad. It was comforting to hear the bears sound off in each of the bedrooms as if in a round. During the busy nighttime routines, I felt grateful and often wondered, "Who was this amazing person who created such a remarkable product to serve families?" I became intrigued and researched articles that shared a glimpse of this innovative female entrepreneur, hoping that one day, I would have the chance to meet her. Awe-inspired, I learned that building bears was her pivoting career move at age 48. I became even more interested in her journey. Inspired, questions flooded my mind. Somehow, she was silently mentoring me, encouraging the idea that we can become whatever we want whenever the time is right and that opportunity for success does not have an expiration date. I also became more patient with myself, focused on my role as CEO of Team Wilkins, and embraced this time. I re-added entrepreneur to my bucket list. After my husband retired from the Army, I became the founder of Team of Seven, LLC.

As our family transitioned to St. Louis for retirement almost fifteen years later, a wish came true! I was able to see the legendary Maxine Clark, founder of the Build-A-Bear Workshop, at several speaking engagements. A mutual friend connected us through email, and she became an advisor and friend. Thank you, Maxine, for being a star in my constellation and creating a loveable product that fosters love and happiness for the world.

Legacies of mentoring

"Tell me and I forget, teach me and I may remember,
involve me and I learn."
—Benjamin Franklin

In 1995, my grandpa, a fully retired accomplished biology teacher, was asked to write in an anthology called *My Folks, The Land of Opportunity*. Once the book was published, he humbly shared the announcement with his family and waved it around the kitchen table. He enticed us to read about our Austrian grandmother, who immigrated from Europe in the late 1800s from the Tyrolean Alps to Chicago and landed in St. Louis. His chapter was called "A Grandma with True Grit." To date, this is one of the only written accounts of our family's stories and how we arrived in the region.

Grandpa's love for learning permeated throughout his character. His focus on education and his excitement surrounding his accomplishment of being a published author resonated with me as I dabbled in various forms of writing in newspaper publications in college and after. I enjoyed writing and imagined that one day, I, too, would be an accomplished, published book author with my own stories to share around the kitchen table. Thank you, Grandpa Litz, for demonstrating the art of the possible and always believing in me. Your inspiration allowed me to check off another item on my bucket list.

Grandpa was a role model in achieving goals in writing and education. He was also inspirational with his hobbies. My great, great-grandmother Ida, had a beautiful singing voice and played the guitar. She was known for her ability to yodel. She brought this gift wherever she went, and it was passed down from generation to generation. Grandpa carried on her legacy and was also a beautiful singer. He sang "Because" at our wedding. He shared his love for boating, golf, bowling, and fly fishing. He passed his love for fly fishing generationally to his great-grandchildren, as he demonstrated to my own sons how to cast and tie flies. He displayed his woodworking abilities by crafting his own fishing net and demonstrated these skills to his grandchildren. He also slalomed behind a boat clear into his seventies just to prove he could, another hobby his grandchildren adopted. He was a role model on many levels, and his legacy has had a ripple effect on all of his grandchildren and great-grandchildren.

As a coach, mentor, teacher, advisor, sponsor, or ally, leading and lifting others to see that light within is essential and the epitome of leadership. These acts create a powerful impact that can last for generations. Mentoring can be considered a holistic approach to long-term development. Yet, many people have short-term mentors that change when situations, positions, and locations change. Mentoring is not ethereal or mysterious. Whether you are mentoring, coaching, or role modeling, one pertinent divine point rings true: the expectation is to give guidance and advice and lead by example.

Who is a mentor?

"Iron sharpens iron, so one person sharpens another."
—Proverbs 27:17

Mentors are everywhere. They show up anytime someone reaches out, answers questions, demonstrates positive behavior, and points you in the right direction. They are in the small, quiet places within our homes and communities, displaying simple role modeling examples. Mentoring can happen in a moment or for a lifetime. It is suggested that we need five to seven mentors throughout life at different times. Each mentor represents a star in a constellation to serve the variety of interests you have in life. Constellations represent the areas where you live, work, and play. Star mentors can be found in schools, churches, neighborhoods, work, hobbies, activities, interest groups, and places where people gather. Silent mentors are those who echo an admired leadership from afar and can leave a remarkable impact on people, even though they have never met. The mentee and mentor relationship is equally important as the role of each is to listen, evoke trust, and create a sense of significance leading to success. Reverse mentoring is extremely important to ignite a practice in interacting between the two parties, and much can be learned from both. In mentoring relationships, iron can sharpen iron.

Parents are one of our first mentors, holding this role for generations as families grow. Teacher, coach, advisor, nurturer, breadwinner, financier, role model, advocate, sponsor, chef, health caregiver, protector, and negotiator are just a few of the roles parents play when raising families. As a mother wearing these hats, I recognize this is the most important role and will mark my career's crowning achievement. Embracing this role sets the foundation for endurance when the trials and tribulations of life happen. This dedication fosters the ability to maneuver through tough times and turns them into triumphs, making a lasting impact on the lives we shape. Parenting is one of the toughest jobs – and hands down the most important. I am reminded of the critical impact we make daily, not only in our professional lives but in our personal lives. This impact shows up in the most interesting and important places through observational learning.

Recently, my oldest daughter and I took the Social Cognitive Career Certification Class together. On the first day of class, she kindly declared to the class that her "mother was her role model and person she looked up to" in one of the opening icebreakers. It is in these moments that we feel seen, appreciated, shocked, humbled, and delighted. It is a memory I will always treasure and not take for granted the important and transformative role of motherhood. Time is one of our most precious commodities. When we give it away, it is a choice. When others give it away, it is a choice. Recognizing others is a way to stop for a moment, reflect on this busy world, and show gratitude. Mentoring is not hard. It is an easy, everyday act where we can emulate service to others by leading, extending our hand, complimenting, or introducing others to people and situations that will bring a positive change in someone's life. In these actions, we lead, lift, and leave a legacy.

Where to find a mentor?

Which mentor's light resonates the most? The mentor within. The true mentor, advisor, or coach required to make the most informative decision – using the mind, faith, intuition, heart, and soul – is YOU. You can have mentors for your entire life, advising you and coaching you one way or another. The goal is to have the propensity, knowledge, self-awareness, and self-efficacy to hear and evaluate these words of wisdom and underscore the ones that resonate with you, your goals, your perspective, your mindset, your vision, your direction, and your faith. Fashioning your own path forward by the guiding lights of coaches, mentors, grandparents, parents, advisors, and others who give you advice is all a part of the process of decision-making. These role models serve as stars that shine and share their light. They are your "board of advisors," championing you to be the best version of yourself. They guide us through our most challenging obstacles and lead us to a destination where significance meets success.

The light within you can flicker, ignite, burn bright, or burn out from the guidance of others. The true mentor is you. It is up to you to light your own journey with the advice and direction sought after and to evaluate from within your own ethical, moral, and directional star map. This requires understanding a true sense of self, knowing your own light, and fueling that flame to ignite the sky to create your own course. For, in the end, it is your race. Hold your own torch, light the path for yourself and others, and "run with perseverance the race that is set before you."

As an entrepreneur, event consultant, speaker, and International Best-Selling Author, Rachel has had a positive influence on thousands of people across the globe, connecting them to resources to improve their career paths in the communities in which they live. Her goal is "to change the world one authentic relationship at a time."

She is the founder and CEO of Team of Seven Consulting, LLC, where she deploys her strategic management and marketing skills to enhance projects, conferences, programming, and events focused in geospatial intelligence and education. Rachel has an International Business background and Interdisciplinary Degree in Business-Marketing, French, and Sociology from the University of Missouri-Columbia (MU) and a foreign language certificate from the University de Grenoble, France. She earned her Executive MBA from Washington University-Saint Louis (WASHU) and holds a certification in the Social Cognitive Career Theory from the National Science Foundation.

As a previous admissions recruiter for MU and WASHU, Rachel understands the power of creating a positive impact for career decisions. Rachel's accolades include the Shield of Sparta and the Dr. Mary E. Walker Award for demonstrating dedicated and exemplary volunteerism improving the quality of life for soldiers and their families. In 2024, she received "Woman of the Year" for Make-A-Wish Missouri-Kansas.

Rachel serves on various boards in the STL Region: John Burroughs Parents Council, SIUE Executive CMIS Advisory Board, Medallion

Adventure Club Executive Board, Folds of Honor Ambassador and Speaker, Women of Wish, and the WASHU Women's Society.

Rachel returned to the region with her husband and five kids after 20 years as a military family. Team Wilkins enjoys the outdoors and seeks adventures in kayaking, skiing, snowboarding, running, hiking, and boating. Her favorite part of life is the time she spends with her family (and her dog Como) during adventures and the holidays.

Please scan the QR code to connect with this author.

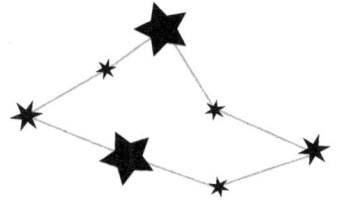

Kristi Borglum

The Power of Authenticity

Life, like water, finds its own path. Sometimes it rushes forward with unstoppable momentum; other times, it moves with quiet persistence, slowly reshaping everything it touches. My journey as a financial advisor, mother, and advocate for authentic leadership has taught me that true strength lies not in resisting these natural flows, but in learning to move with them while staying true to your core.

My journey into the financial services industry wasn't a straight path, but it was paved with the values instilled by my entrepreneurial family. Growing up with two brothers, we weren't just given opportunities—we were given responsibilities. Our parents ensured we had everything we needed: annual family vacations, sports activities, and extracurricular pursuits. These privileges also came with expectations. On the weekends in middle school, you'd find us rolling newspapers in the garage at 3 a.m., the rhythmic sound of work and Motown becoming our earliest business education and flow. We learned the art of commercial cleaning, mastering everything from industrial floor buffers to deep-cleaning carpets to maneuvering electric waste caddies. Managing newspaper route billing taught us about customer service and financial responsibility. These weren't just paid chores; they were lessons in perseverance, attention to detail, and the value of consistent and persistent effort. Our family believed in the honor of hard work, regardless of the task every job was treated with dedication. These early experiences shaped my understanding that success isn't measured by the prestige of your position or the financial achievement, but by the effort you bring to it. These lessons in respect, integrity, frugality, and honor later became the cornerstone of my professional philosophy.

After college, feeling the pull toward personal growth, I made the bold decision to spend a year in Hawaii. This wasn't just a young person's adventure—it was my declaration of independence, a statement that I could navigate any waters I chose to enter. That confidence would serve me well in the years to come, though life would soon teach me that true strength isn't always about powering through life's obstacles—sometimes it's about learning to flow around them.

This lesson came into sharp focus when my husband Kyle and I faced the challenges of raising children who experience the world differently. Behind our picture-perfect family photos lay a reality that required us to completely reimagine our approach to parenting. Our son's struggles with big emotions, energy, and impulse control initially felt overwhelming. I fought against it at first, trying to maintain control and meet others' expectations of what our family "should" look like. The breakthrough came when we realized that our children's differences weren't limitations—they were invitations to discover new ways of supporting and nurturing their unique potential. We built a comprehensive network of support—pediatricians, parent coaches, psychologists, psychiatrists, functional medicine doctors, chiropractors, teachers, counselors, and even our beloved dog, Dexter. Each plays a vital role in helping our children thrive. This journey taught me a fundamental truth that would transform my personal and professional life: you don't have to be all things to all people. You are already enough. Sometimes the strongest thing you can do is ask for help.

Entering the financial services industry, where only 23% of CFP®️ professionals are women, presented its own set of challenges. Early in my career, after having to miss a prospect call while caring for my toddler and six-month-old, someone told me that "some people just aren't made for business development." I also remember stories of the most "successful" female advisors who chose to cut their generous maternity leave short to prioritize the business. Those words and stories could have defined my path, but instead, they fueled my determination to succeed on my own terms. The real transformation began in 2020 when I re-joined Moneta as an advisor. Initially, I approached the role with lingering doubts about my ability to attract new clients. Something remarkable happened when I stopped trying to fit the traditional mold of what a financial advisor "should" be. My natural inclination toward emotional intelligence, combined with technical expertise and genuine care for clients' well-being, turned out to be exactly what many families were looking for. What I once saw as limitations—being a mother who sometimes needs to prioritize family, or approaching client relationships from a place of nurturing rather than pure sales—became my greatest strengths. Business development, which once terrified me, has become one of my favorite aspects of the role. Not because I changed who I was, but because I finally embraced it.

This professional evolution paralleled another important journey—my relationship with alcohol. Like many professionals, my drinking habits were socially acceptable and never interfered with my productivity or work. Yet something inside me recognized that I wasn't bringing my best self to my family, my clients, or myself. Through therapy and deep self-reflection—the hardest but most rewarding work—I chose sobriety. I'm currently on my second sobriety journey, and this time it's fundamentally different. After my first fifteen months of sobriety, I convinced myself

I could manage occasional drinking—special occasions only. As anyone who's walked this path knows, "special occasions" have a way of multiplying. What started as vacation-only drinks expanded to sunny Fridays, pool days, and social gatherings. While my drinking remained within socially acceptable bounds, I noticed subtle shifts in myself: diminished sleep quality, reduced focus, shorter patience with my children, and a general dulling of my clarity and motivation. These changes might not have been noticed by others, but I felt them. The decision to return to sobriety wasn't driven by any external crisis or pressure—it came from a deep recognition and self-observation that I wanted more for myself, my family, and my clients. This time, I'm not trying to prove anything to anyone, including myself. I'm simply choosing a clearer path forward, and I feel great about it. The transformation has been profound but quiet. Like the gentle persistence of water-shaping stone, sobriety has gradually enhanced every aspect of my life. My sleep is deeper, my thinking sharper, my presence with my children more complete. In client meetings, I bring a level of focus and emotional attunement that allows me to truly understand not just their financial goals, but their deeper motivations and concerns. These qualities don't just make me a better parent and person— they make me a better advisor. The journey has taught me that sometimes our greatest growth comes not from adding something to our lives, but from having the courage to let something go. Sobriety isn't about deprivation; it's about choosing clarity, authenticity, and presence over temporary comfort or social conformity.

The intersection of personal growth and professional success has taught me that authenticity isn't just about being true to yourself—it's about creating spaces where others can do the same. In my practice, I've found that clients are drawn to advisors who bring their whole selves to the relationship. They want someone who understands that financial decisions aren't just about numbers—they're about hopes, fears, dreams, and family legacies. For women navigating the financial planning profession, I offer this truth: your authentic self is your greatest asset. Build a practice that aligns with your values rather than trying to fit someone else's mold. Partner with mentors who believe in your potential, even when you're still growing into it. The future of financial planning needs more diverse voices and perspectives. We need leaders who understand that technical expertise and emotional intelligence aren't mutually exclusive, and that the best client relationships are built on trust, understanding, and genuine connection.

Sometimes this means being honest about our limitations—yes, there are times when my children need me more than a prospect call, and that's okay. What matters is building authentic relationships with clients who understand and appreciate these values. At Moneta, I found colleagues who recognized and valued what makes me unique as an advisor: my genuine love for people, high emotional intelligence, analytical capabilities, and the drive and experience to back it all up.

As I continue evolving both personally and professionally, I'm committed to being the kind of leader and mentor I needed when I was starting out—one who proves that success doesn't require compromising who you are or what matters most. My journey has shown me that our perceived limitations often become our greatest strengths when we have the courage to embrace them fully. Every challenge I've faced—from parenting to sobriety to building my practice—has reinforced this truth: authenticity isn't just an aspiration, it's a superpower.

The journey to authenticity requires courage. It means facing our fears, acknowledging our struggles, and being willing to show up imperfectly. My path—from early morning paper routes to Hawaiian adventures, from parenting challenges to professional triumphs, from drinking to sobriety—has taught me that our perceived limitations often become our greatest strengths when we have the courage to embrace them fully. To those navigating their own paths in business and life, I offer this: Trust the flow of your journey. Your unique experiences, challenges, and perspective aren't obstacles to success—they're the very things that will set you apart. Build your support network but remember that the most important supporter is yourself. Make choices that align with your values, even when they don't fit the traditional mold.

Like water, we all find our own way forward. Sometimes we rush forward with unstoppable momentum; other times, we move with quiet persistence, slowly reshaping everything we touch. The key is to stay true to your course while remaining fluid enough to adapt to life's changing currents. Your authenticity is your superpower. Use it to create meaningful change in your family, your industry, your community, and your world. Every challenge you face is an opportunity to demonstrate that success doesn't require compromising who you are or what matters most. Your story, your struggles, your strengths—they all matter.

Like a river carving its path through the landscape, your authenticity has the power to reshape everything it touches, creating something beautiful and uniquely yours.

As a Senior Advisor at Moneta, Kristi serves as a trusted partner helping clients navigate all areas of their financial lives through genuine connection and relationship growth. She strives to take the burden of worry off clients' minds so they can focus on what matters most.

Kristi earned her BSBA with an emphasis on Finance and a minor in Economics from the University of Missouri – Columbia. She obtained the CERTIFIED FINANCIAL PLANNER™ designation in 2016 and continues to refine her education and skills to help clients succeed. She is passionate about leadership and believes being your authentic self is your greatest asset.

Outside of Moneta, Kristi enjoys a constant on-the-go lifestyle with her partner and two young children. She focuses on growing valuable relationships with family, friends, clients, and community, which tend to mix together in one beautiful tribe.

Please scan the QR code to connect with this author.

Ali Carson

Be the Mentor You Needed

"Live. Laugh. Love. Learn. Leave a Legacy."
— Beccy Baldwin (aka Mom)

I've been so very blessed to have worked with some amazing leaders over the course of my career, but a few made an impact I will carry with me forever. Not only because they were exceptional leaders but because they didn't just lead; they mentored, supported, advocated, and trusted. They were the mentors I needed to shape me into the leader and professional woman I am today. I hope this chapter serves to not only honor them but also to share some of their wisdom.

"Leadership is about making others better as a result of your presence,
and making sure that impact lasts in your absence."
— Sheryl Sandberg

Randy

When we first moved to St. Louis, I went to a staffing agency to help me find a job. Randy not only offered to help; he hired me himself. I started working as an Office Coordinator, but I knew I wanted to do more. Randy gave me the opportunity to work as a Direct Hire Recruiter—and I was terrible at it! I loved working with the candidates but hated cold-calling companies to try to convince them to hire my candidate. I just couldn't bring myself to do it, and it's hard to be successful in this type of role without focusing on sales.

After months of chances and support in every shape and form, Randy made the correct choice to let me go. I can still remember sitting in his office. I even remember the suit I was wearing during that conversation.

I remember two things most of all...

1. The utter horror of realizing I had failed at something. This was a first. I was your stereotypical straight-A student, valedictorian, high achiever. Failure was not only not an option; it wasn't even in my vocabulary. I had failed at my first real job out of graduate school, and it gutted me.

2. The way Randy treated me with such dignity and respect. The way he handled the whole situation taught me that you can do your job as a leader and address performance issues in a way that is respectful and maintains the person's dignity. Even 20 years later, he remains a leader I speak of fondly because of how he handled the situation.

Ultimately, I look back on this experience with gratitude, because I learned from it. I learned that it's ok to fail. It's not only ok but also normal. I learned that failing is something that you can and will recover from. I learned about the kind of leader I wanted to be.

Janet

Janet hired me as the eighth employee of a brand-new hospital. I knew from the first interview (which lasted about twice as long as it was supposed to) that we would be a great partnership. Janet is everything a leader should be. She is smart, dedicated, but most importantly truly invested in helping her team develop and grow. She naturally approaches her leadership from an authentic and strengths-based perspective. This significantly shaped my own approach to leadership.

One of my favorite parts of working with Janet was that she wasn't worried about what was on my actual job description but instead focused on what work I was passionate about doing and that aligned with my natural talents. She gave me opportunities to train and coach others even though that wasn't part of my job at the time. She allowed me to come alongside her and learn, giving me the opportunity to develop a depth of expertise in the HR space that I didn't have previously. Best of all, she created a team and an environment where we had a lot of fun. I learned that work doesn't feel as much like work when you're doing what you love with people who are doing the same.

The growth I had in the five years I worked for Janet was transformative. While I didn't realize it at the time, Janet's strengths-based approach taught me to seek out the strengths in others and laid the foundation for my later focus on helping people discover and live their strengths.

Krista

When I first talked to Krista about a job opening on her team, I didn't meet the qualifications for the role. I had been doing training and coaching but had not been a formal people manager, which was initially listed as a requirement. Fortunately, Krista could see the potential in me and took the chance to hire me anyway. Her willingness to do so fully changed the trajectory of my career.

Krista recognized my potential to excel in teaching leadership development. She recognized a passionate student. She understood that she could teach the skills needed to be successful, but she couldn't teach the passion that I naturally brought to the role. Krista taught me to trust my gut, to look for potential in others, and to invest in the potential you find. Through her guidance, I discovered the joy of taking a chance on others and being fully invested in their success, just as she did for me.

LaurieGrace

LaurieGrace and I met by chance at our first training class to become Gallup-Certified Strengths Coaches. I was so convicted hearing her speak so eloquently about developing others during our session I convinced her to have lunch with me. This allowed me to soak up more of her wisdom delivered in the sweetest Texas accent. A year later, we found ourselves in the same session again at our second class, and by the third, we planned to attend together. We also met each year at Gallup's annual conference, carving out time for dinners, drinks, and catching up. Every time we got together, I wished I had a pen to capture her insights. She was about 10 years ahead of me on her coaching journey and I wanted to learn all I could from her. She gave her wisdom freely and sought guidance from me as well. Our give-and-take has become one of my favorite things.

When I made the decision to launch my own coaching and consulting business, I called up LaurieGrace once again to pick her brain about starting a business. What did she do at the beginning that really worked well? What did she wish she had done? What were some of her greatest lessons learned? In true LG fashion, she shared her experiences authentically, transparently, and fully. There were no silly questions or off-limits topics. She was more than willing to share. She prayed with me and for me as I was navigating this next step in my journey, as she had for so many other steps along the way. What I found in reflecting on those conversations was the realization that there is no one "right" way to run a business, to be a coach, to be successful. In our conversations, I found permission to create my own definition of success and pursue it with passion.

Beccy

I've written before about lessons I learned from my mother, Beccy, and the impact she had on the woman I've become. I haven't shared how she was, in many ways, my North Star and the bar I measure myself against. There were so many times over the course of my career I would call my mother up. Sometimes I needed to vent frustration, to cry out my hurt, but most often it was to help me get unstuck. Whether I was navigating a particularly tough time in parenthood or a challenging situation at work, I always knew she was just a phone call away with the guidance I needed.

I always had a sense that she was a bit of a big deal in her field, but it wasn't until she passed away that I fully appreciated the impact she had on the world of education. She was a trailblazer, an advocate, a mentor, and a friend who inspired others to achieve more than they thought was possible, just like she did for my sisters and me. In hearing their stories at her funeral and after, one thought kept running through my head. It's one I continue to repeat and the bar I now measure myself against. *"If I make a fraction of the impact she had on the world, I'll be a success."*

> *"It's been true in my life that when I've needed a mentor,*
> *the right person shows up."*
> —Ken Blanchard

There are lessons we can take away from every experience. I didn't start relationships with any of these leaders seeking mentors. By sharing themselves authentically, these leaders *became* the mentors I needed. As I reflect on my own career journey and the legacy I hope to leave, I see their influence reflected in the lessons I leave you now:

- **Failing is ok**—even encouraged. It's how we learn and grow.
- **Authenticity matters**. Your unique gifts are exactly what the world needs.
- **Take a chance**—even if results aren't guaranteed. You never know until you try.
- **Share generously**. There's plenty of opportunity for everyone and no room for a scarcity mindset.

- **Be present.** Whether someone needs guidance, advice, or just a listening ear, you never know when a simple conversation might unlock their next big insight.
- **Show unwavering faith in people.** Everyone needs a champion cheering them on.

I am eternally grateful for every lesson these mentors imparted. Grateful for the tough conversations, for the unwavering belief in my potential, and for the gentle push to find my own path. Their examples taught me that mentorship is the ultimate gift; it transcends roles and titles, leaving behind an enduring ripple of growth.

In your own journey, you have the same opportunity: to be the mentor you once needed, to invest in others as boldly as someone once invested in you, and to create the kind of impact that lingers long after you've left the room. Ultimately, I believe *that* is how we *lead, lift, and leave a legacy.*

Ali Carson, MBA, ACC, is a #1 international best-selling author, experienced coach, and dynamic facilitator with two decades of experience in human resources, leadership development, and team effectiveness.

As the Founder and CEO of Movere Coaching, LLC, Ali helps high-achieving professionals and organizations unlock their strengths, lead with authenticity, and create thriving workplaces. She is a Gallup-Certified Strengths Coach, a Results-Certified Brain-Based Coach, and holds the Associate Certified Coach (ACC) credential through the ICF. She brings tools founded in neuroscience to her strengths-based approach to create impactful coaching and learning experiences for her clients. Before launching Movere Coaching, she held senior talent development roles in both the healthcare and legal industries.

Outside of work, Ali is a wife, mother to two teenagers, and sister. She enjoys exploring nature through camping trips in the family RV, filled with hiking, paddleboarding, and discovering great local restaurants.

Please scan the QR code to connect with this author.

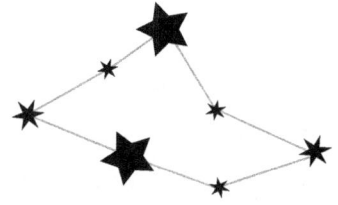

Aukje Rijpkema

The Wind at My Back

Following my first day working outside the home in eight years, I walked into a silent, empty house. This was vastly different from the reception I'd prepared for my husband for nearly a decade after we put my career on hold to support his. There was no one waiting for me, no kiss on my cheek, no dinner on the table, no one to ask how my day went. At that moment, I'd never felt more alone...

It was also the day after my husband packed up and left me, our family, and the life we'd built together for nearly 30 years. I fell on the sofa sobbing. How in the world did it come to this? Would I ever manage to let go of these overwhelming feelings of sadness?

We met in high school in 1991 in The Netherlands, our home country, and went to college there together. While he earned his master's degree, I paid the bills, working at a pharmaceutical company. Under guidance from my mentor, I built my first computer programs, predicting warehouse sizes and drafting layouts. My mentor was the first one to believe in me and to propel me forward.

When the opportunity for jobs in Seattle for both of us arose, we got married. It was a quick wedding, held just three weeks after a flying visit to a city we'd never been to before. We found a wonderful place to live and had the time of our lives in Seattle—full time jobs, paychecks, parties, freedom. It was there, at Romac Industries, where I took a deep dive into data, working with Oracle databases and Enterprise applications. I earned the same salary as the receptionist but was grateful to have a job. I learned fast and was soon indispensable. My paycheck adjusted accordingly. Most importantly, I loved my job! The greatest lessons that CIO taught me were to be very meticulous when making changes to applications and every customization is costly down the line, so aim to stay as 'vanilla' as possible. We worked closely together; he had my back and to this day believes in me.

My husband and I moved back to The Netherlands when we were ready to have children. I found a job with what is now a Canon company. I dug into SAP's Business Suite and, soon after, SAP's Business Warehouse. I was working part time, and at first hesitated to sign my contract because I was pregnant. Pregnancy leave is 16 weeks in The Netherlands. I wondered if they'd still hire me if they knew. I asked my boss, the only woman manager at the time. She smiled and said of course it wouldn't be a problem. Sign! She lifted me up then and has continued to do so—as both a role model and a friend.

During this time, our daughter was born, and soon after, our son. My husband's responsibilities grew, he traveled more, even lived abroad part-time, working long days and coming home exhausted. When he was asked to move our family to Hong Kong, I said, after some consideration, "Yes!" Knowing by then that my willingness to embrace new opportunities would benefit me in the long run.

The small island on which we lived with many other expats was beautiful. Every day felt like vacation. The kids, by then aged 6 and 7, made friends quickly with the other Dutch kids at school. A live-in nanny did all the house chores while I kept working remotely on my own terms for another three years. Life was one big adventure!

We had known the day would come that we would be asked to move back to the United States, where corporate headquarters were located. Changing our lives again, we traded Hong Kong for St. Louis. It was at that point I decided to quit my job. We didn't have an extended expat family, like we did in Hong Kong. There was no network to rely upon. Distances were much less compact than on the island and getting anything done took time. The kids had to be driven to and from school every day. My family depended on me being available to make sure everything ran smoothly at home and for my husband to focus 100% on work. Life was different, but good, and the future looked bright.

Taking care of our big suburban house, my family, the dogs, the yard, driving from carpool lane to carpool lane, and volunteering at school kept me more than busy. I was grateful to be the rock of the family, keeping it all together. I didn't mind putting off my own ambitions, because after all, we were a team.

It wasn't all glorious. The kids struggled at first, missing their old friends and finding it hard to make new ones. By then, they had lived on three different continents, while most of their classmates' families had lived in St. Louis for generations. Our kids were strangers. Once they made it into high school, things got better. The kids did well in school, and we took long family vacations because we could. My husband would join us in short bursts. Meanwhile, his profile at work continued to skyrocket and his job was ever more demanding.

My kids couldn't wait to get their driver's licenses. As soon as they did, I really got my freedom back. It had been 7 years of being a wife and a mother first and foremost. I was excited and very ready to start doing something big for myself again. Over the summer of 2019, I spotted a six-month data analytics bootcamp at Washington University in St. Louis. It was exactly what I'd been looking for. I applied and spent every free hour working diligently through the course material and exercises. It was all coming back to me, plus so much more. I loved it!

Then the global pandemic hit. Slowly the virus crept around the globe and into our lives. Schools switched to remote learning, as did my classes. When the world started to crumble, so did my marriage. I didn't see it quite as clearly then as I do now. I was very focused on graduating from the rigorous program and re-entering the workforce. During the summer of 2020, the children and I returned home to The Netherlands, where I applied for jobs back in St. Louis. Something felt different, but then again, the whole world did.

One of my classmates at Washington University was the CTO at Clayco, a 'design build construction company' in St. Louis. He encouraged me to apply for a Business Intelligence Developer role that opened up. I knew this position would be perfect for me! I went through seven interviews and convinced them I was the right person for the job. When asked how much I'd like to be paid, I said, 'I don't care, I just want the job!' I was confident the rest would follow, which it did. I was so excited to be back in the workforce. That CTO was constantly looking for new technologies to support our business from different angles. He taught me much about the construction industry and to think outside the box.

Though I knew we were going through a rough patch in our marriage, I didn't fully realize how off it was until I returned to St. Louis, ready to start my new job. My husband told me that he needed space to live on his own. All I could do was stand there, totally flabbergasted, and nod. After 30 years of being together, he gathered his stuff and left…

Years later, I realized how much the universe kept bringing people into my life at just the right time, providing the wind I needed to fly. First, though, I had to work through the hard parts and reinvent myself. I had been a 'we' since I was 19 years old and considered myself part of a team, working toward shared goals. Here I was, living in St. Louis, far away from family, with two kids about to finish high school and a husband who had literally checked out. Who was I now? How could I reclaim the parts of myself that I had lost or given up?

As it turned out, my first manager at Clayco saw potential in me. He lifted me up, both professionally and emotionally, supporting me through the first tough months. I leaned deep into Clayco's business processes, applications, and people. I felt a strong sense of fighting my way towards my new life. Work was my anchor, where I felt validated and seen. I picked up work where I could, and it paid off. After only a few months, I received my first promotion. I focused on aligning data and reporting, while working with all facets of the business, building relationships and trust.

Life continued to be too busy to stand still. The company's focus on data led to a separate data team. A Vice President was hired, and people were added from other parts of the IT organization. Our CIO believed in me, and I was promoted again, this time to Manager of Data & Analytics. My team, and responsibilities, grew. Our data strategy took flight as we built out more reporting based on a robust enterprise data warehouse.

Clayco's VP of Data & Engineering, to whom I reported, recommended me for an IT leadership program. I felt honored to attend and learned numerous soft skills. I was also assigned a mentor, the CIO at another company, with whom I met monthly. Serendipitously, he was also Dutch. He taught me much about influencing, gaining trust and the human side of the work we do. Both of them have had my back and moved me forward.

After some time, a new female VP was hired. She was super smart, had a calm demeanor with a plethora of experience. She led by example, taught me many leadership skills, lifted me up and mentored me in too many ways to describe.

During the two years following her joining Clayco, my team would more than double in size. We now were a group of Data Scientists, Business Intelligence Analysts and a couple of overseas consultants. Time flew, and four years into the job, I was promoted once more. This time into a director's role. Growing my responsibilities and team in size again. And just like before, it all happened at exactly the right time!

While all this was going on, life behind the scenes moved on as well, I got divorced, moved both kids into wonderful colleges, single handedly sold the St. Louis house and most of the stuff in it, started a brand-new life in Chicago, where I bought a beautiful condo in the heart of the city, and moved over what was left of my old life.

Looking in the rearview mirror, what seemed disastrous and unmanageable at first has turned out to be a tremendous blessing and gift. I had to reinvent myself, and found that the more I leaned back, the more the universe provided the wind at my back. There's so much gratitude in my heart for the people that have and continue to lift me up. I am 100% intent on returning the favor and passing on what I have been given, hoping to leave a legacy of my own along the way.

Aukje Rijpkema was born and raised in The Netherlands, the oldest of three girls. Growing up, she lived next to the manufacturing plant that was owned and managed by her father, from whom she inherited her inquisitive nature and resilience when facing life's challenges. Her mother instilled the creative side in her. Aukje is the proud mother of 2 witty young adults.

Her sisters have been her biggest blessing and stoutest supporters, but she also developed a devoted group of friends around the world while living on three continents and in four U.S. states. Aukje has shared many experiences and adventures with them, and they regularly reciprocated her own efforts as mentors, therapists, and confidants. She's forever grateful for having all these women in her life.

Aukje enjoys an active lifestyle, including participating in beautiful hikes and challenging races across the globe, with the 2024 marathon in her adopted hometown of Chicago being the most recent.

Please scan the QR code to connect with this author.

Tina Linnenbrink

Seeds of Wisdom

The Roots of Mentorship

Mentoring is like planting bamboo—a process that demands patience, faith, and persistence. For months, even years, you water the seed, tend the soil, and trust in something you cannot see. Above ground, there's no sign of progress, no proof that your efforts are making a difference. Beneath the surface, an intricate root system is forming, strengthening, and preparing. Then, in its time, the bamboo rises—not rushed, but with quiet wisdom, shaped by patience and unseen growth.

Wisdom works the same way. The insights we share may not spark an instant transformation, but they settle quietly, waiting for the right moment to take hold. A single piece of advice, a passing word of encouragement—these can be the roots of confidence, resilience, and bold action later on.

I was fortunate. Throughout my youth and career, extraordinary women planted these seeds within me—nurturing my potential, offering guidance, and extending patience when I fumbled. For years, I absorbed their lessons without fully realizing it. Then, one day, I looked up and saw how far I had grown.

Early Lessons from My Mother

Growing up, my mother (and first unofficial mentor) often shared simple but thoughtful nuggets of wisdom during tough childhood moments. She'd say things like, **"To thy self be true"** or **"You get what you give"**, without elaborating on their meaning. Instead, she trusted that these phrases would resonate with me as I grew older and that, over time, I would reflect and apply them to my personal experiences. Her timing was always intentional, striking a balance between guiding me and letting me learn on my own. While I didn't always realize it then, those words shaped how I navigated challenges as I entered the workforce, and even now, their impact lingers. A childhood friend once reminded me of how I'd shared my mother's words of wisdom with her, proving how far-reaching her subtle guidance had been—not just for me, but for others.

Seeds of Strength:

In 1997, I accepted a job offer to move from my small rural hometown in Illinois to the East Coast, more than 1200 miles from family and friends. This was a challenge and an opportunity because I would be stepping into a bigger role at the headquarters of a large global conglomerate. While I was excited about the opportunity, I was equally nervous, fearing failure (the feeling could be described as imposter syndrome). My previous mentor had recommended me for the position, although I had little relevant experience—just a strong dose of tenacity, curiosity, and ambition. My new manager, Wendy, was the Vice President of Organizational Development and had an intriguing background with degrees in both journalism and horticulture. Ha! Looking back, I can only imagine the shock she must've felt reading my first few attempts at corporate communications!

From day one, Wendy spent time getting to know me personally. The first few months, she took me to lunch weekly and invited me to her home for dinner to meet her husband and daughter. She asked me to complete small projects to watch how I processed information and completed assignments. This level of investment is rare in today's workplace, but looking back, it allowed her to understand my learning style. Wendy learned my strengths and weaknesses, how I processed information, and what motivated and demotivated me. Just as my mother had planted seeds of wisdom with patience and intention, Wendy did the same. She wasn't just a manager; she was a continuation of the mentorship I had known all my life, reinforcing the kind of thoughtful guidance that shaped both my career and character.

Seeds of Wisdom at Work

One of the most impactful lessons came early in my new role. A senior HR executive voiced concerns to Wendy about my ability to meet deadlines and communicate effectively. When Wendy relayed his feedback, I felt defeated and defensive. I had worked hard, never missed a deadline, and believed the criticism was unfair. Wendy stopped me and first told me she believed me. Then, she shared these powerful words: **"Sometimes, Tina, you have to fight power with power."** I felt immediate relief, but also confusion. I felt relieved because she believed me, but also confused—what did that even mean? She guided me on how to present facts, not feelings, by gathering documentation of conversations and creating a timeline with dates. Because she trusted me, I felt empowered to respond to inaccurate accusations and felt confident that the information I included on the timeline would resolve the issue. This lesson was incredibly valuable. I learned that **power isn't about position or dominance**; it's about presenting factual evidence to support a side and gaining the support of someone who can vouch for integrity and work ethic.

I experienced many defining moments that reshaped my approach to leadership and problem-solving. I distinctly recall another coaching moment from Wendy when I was frustrated by a leader's repeated bad behavior. I walked into her office, fired up and ready to unload a list of complaints, expecting swift action. She was a VP, and he was "just" a Director. I thought Wendy would wave her corporate wand and fix everything instantly. Instead, she calmly met my frustration and said, **"Sometimes, Tina, you have to let the process work itself out."** Annoyed, I was disappointed she wasn't ready to take quick action. What I didn't realize was that she already knew about the situation and had involved the SVP of HR, legal, and divisional senior leadership behind the scenes. What felt like inaction to me was a thoughtful, strategic approach. That moment taught me another valuable lesson: **trust the process.** Not every issue requires an immediate crusade for justice. Sometimes, you must resist the urge to play corporate superhero and let policies, investigations, and established processes do their work. It's not about being passive. It's about being smart, staying professional, and letting cooler, more experienced heads prevail. Spoiler alert: the issue did get resolved—and yes, the jerk was fired.

Mentorship Through Clear Communication

Wendy's wisdom didn't stop there. Among the many lessons she instilled in me, one that reshaped how I communicate—both personally and professionally—was that being understood is just as important as being right. One particularly hectic day at work, I was attempting to explain something to Wendy, convinced I was making perfect sense. As I went on, she asked several questions that didn't make sense to me, so I stopped her, frustrated, and blurted out, "Wendy, you're not listening to me." She paused, met my eyes with the kindest, most patient look, and said gently, **'No, Tina—you aren't explaining it clearly.'** That moment hit me like a ton of bricks—bricks that built a foundation of humility. It was a complete shift in how I viewed my ability to communicate effectively.

I reflected on that comment for days and realized that being a good communicator isn't about how well *I think* I'm explaining something—it's about how clearly the other person understands it (sounds simple, but not everyone gets it). After gaining a different perspective, I started paying closer attention to people's expressions, reactions, and questions to gauge whether they truly understood what I was saying. Her feedback didn't just make me a better communicator at work—it reshaped how I approach conversations with family and friends. Here is the irony: I mentioned my manager was a journalism and horticulture manager, so she knew a thing or two about clear communication and **"*pruning*"** away what wasn't working.

The Legacy of Mentorship

When Wendy showed me how to *"Fight power with power,"* she taught me to advocate for myself with confidence and strategy, not emotion. When she reminded me to *"Let the process work itself out,"* she helped me see that leadership requires patience, trust, and the humility to accept that I can't control everything. And when she gently corrected me with, *"You aren't explaining it clearly,"* she made me realize that great communication isn't about being right—it's about being understood.

Wendy's wisdom over the three years I was blessed to work with her helped shape me into a more thoughtful, strategic, and emotionally intelligent leader—even when it was tough to hear. She didn't sugarcoat reality or shield me from uncomfortable truths. She pushed me to rise above my frustrations, see situations from a broader perspective, and take responsibility for my actions and communication. Wendy didn't just teach me how to navigate challenges—she taught me how to grow through them, becoming the kind of leader who could one day mentor others in the same powerful way.

Sadly, at the young age of 44, Wendy passed away. I was devasted! I had lost my cheerleader and the one person I could call for advice when a difficult situation arose. Because I had grown so close to Wendy, her husband asked if I would say a few words about her at her funeral service. As I contemplated what I would say, all I could think was, "How am I going to be successful without her?" But, during that time of reflection, I decided to take a different approach, and instead, I would ask myself, "What would Wendy do?" and her seeds of wisdom would ring in my ears.

Sowing It Forward

Over the years, I've met amazing young women who are eager to learn and have so much talent. I look for opportunities to pass on Wendy's legacy by planting seeds of wisdom with those who are open, hoping that one day, the seeds will take root and cultivate a strong foundation for their growth.

Tina is a seasoned HR executive, mentor, and entrepreneur with over twenty years of experience transforming HR in manufacturing, healthcare, transportation, and retail. She has designed and implemented HR departments from the ground up, turning them into high-performing, strategic functions that drive business success. Passionate about developing HR professionals, she mentors them to grow, excel, and achieve their career aspirations. As a certified DDI International facilitator, she thrives on developing leaders and fostering high-performing teams.

She launched SRVHR to help small, growth-focused businesses thrive by implementing proven talent strategies and scalable HR systems that drive sustainable success. With deep expertise in HR transformation, she ensures companies have the right people strategies to achieve their goals.

Her mentoring experience extends to her sister, a 30-year traumatic brain injury survivor. Coaching her through daily routines has strengthened Tina's resilience and coaching mindset. She also enjoys spending time with her husband, daughter, and stepsons, embracing family adventures and meaningful moments together.

Please scan the QR code to connect with this author.

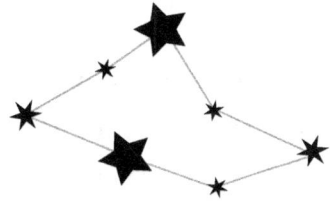

Sara Ward

The Art of Blooming

*"A flower does not think of competing with the
flower next to it. It just blooms".*
—Sensei Ogui

I can't remember exactly when my love for flowers began, whether in my grandmother's garden, my mother's paintings, or my sister's weddings. I have always had a deep profound appreciation for them.

Growing up in St. Louis, I have fond memories of our large suburban yard, complete with a massive magnolia tree and grand columns adorning the front of our home. My mother had a passion for art, cooking, gardening, and entertaining. I vividly recall the many dinner parties she hosted. Pulling out the fine china, crystal, and silverware to set a beautiful table. My father's house was no different when it came to weddings, holiday gatherings, and family dinners.

When I moved in with my dad and stepmom, I was thrilled because I got to choose my bed comforter and curtains. I selected an abstract floral print in soothing oceanic colors. At my mom's house, my room was decorated with a rainbow-themed comforter, complete with matching pillows. As an artist and interior designer, she went a step further and painted a rainbow on my wall, ending in a heart. This was where my love for color began. I cherished the joy of creativity —whether it was decorating my room, experimenting with fashion, or even cooking.

Like any teenager, I wanted to be loved and accepted while figuring out who I was. I also craved attention, especially from boys. School was a struggle for me from an early age, and I spent a lot of time in resource rooms. However, in junior high and high school, I had many wonderful teachers. One of them, Dr. Franklin, encouraged me to get expressive with my assignments, such as drawing historical scenes to represent what we were studying. Through his class, I developed a love for history. He once told me that I was smart and capable of achieving great things. It was one of the first times I can remember anyone expressing a belief in my academic abilities, and it made a lasting impact. Over time, I've realized that I'm a very visual learner, and the traditional classroom didn't suit my learning style.

Beginning to Blossom

After high school, I struggled to decide what to do with my life. College felt like the natural next step. My dad suggested pursuing a business degree, which could lead to many career paths. I leaned toward fashion and design as a career. One college recruiter even suggested a career as a fashion buyer for a department store, but for reasons I can't recall, I didn't pursue it. Instead, we decided I'd start with an associate's degree at community college and see where it led. I almost finished but couldn't pass math and biology, leaving me just shy of three classes from my degree.

During those years, I was always searching for something—a purpose, a sense of belonging. Faith had been a part of my upbringing; my family attended church when my parents were married, and even after their divorce, my mom continued to take me to church during my school years. After high school, I stopped attending church for about five years.

At that time, I worked full-time and lived on my own. I had friends, but often felt lost. One day, a coworker whose husband was in seminary invited me to her church. It was more formal than I was accustomed to. She introduced me to another church, which was a new church plant in the city. From the moment I attended, I fell in love with it. This church was unlike any I had experienced before. It emphasized that we don't need to have it all together or be perfect to be loved and accepted by God. Jesus captured my heart in a way I had never known.

This church also focused on reconciliation across racial divides—something I had never thought deeply about before. It opened my eyes to issues of injustice, poverty, and the richness of Black culture. I developed a love for learning about different cultures and hearing stories from people whose experiences differed from my own. These lessons have shaped me and continue to inspire how I see the world and my place in it.

During my time at this church, I met a man who listened to me and made me laugh. Later, this funny man would become my husband. He was someone I could trust and, for the first time in my life, be myself.

Our first year of marriage was an adjustment. I was learning to live with a person with a different background and perspective. At our church, we were friends with an older couple who soon became our mentors. It was so great to have people to talk to about life, marriage, and parenting. Almost thirty years later, this couple is still a special part of our lives. My greatest advice to newly married couples is to have a couple who has been in a loving marriage for many years. They have helped us work through difficulties and normal life challenges. It takes great effort to have a great marriage.

We enjoyed having people over for meals. My husband was a pastor at our church and family was the center of our lives. I learned to cook from scratch and savored the creativity it gave me. Martha Stewart was someone I admired. She made everyday life beautiful. Her weddings always made me think outside the box, especially the beautiful flowers. I admired how she showed others how to create stunning celebrations. Friends began asking me to cater for their weddings and do their flowers. The planning and execution of the process were my favorite part.

While I was so grateful for the opportunity to stay home with our three children while they were young, I always needed something for myself. I enjoyed working part-time. I worked at Wildflowers while I was pregnant with our youngest. During my time there, my husband's job moved us to several places, including Philadelphia. While there, I worked at a local high-end florist. That experience deepened my appreciation for flowers and beautiful events. My boss was a great mentor, teaching me how to design flowers and run a business.

After Philadelphia, we moved to Lima, Peru. This deepened my love for culture. Living in Peru was one of the greatest experiences I've ever had. I cherished the culture that focused on relationships, where people came first before agendas or efficiency. I learned to listen, to be present, and to enjoy the moment. After our time in Peru ended abruptly, we returned to St. Louis. This was the last place I wanted to be. I felt like my whole identity was lost. I had been someone who lived internationally and had started a jewelry business for at-risk teenage moms. I struggled with how to rebuild my life and my family's life.

Blooming Where You Are Planted

Back in St. Louis, we returned to our church where my husband was on staff as a pastor. We enrolled our kids in school and found a house. I used my leadership gifts to help with large events at our church and outreach ministries. I ended up working with the food ministry, where we fed hundreds of meals each day to at-risk kids. I relished planning meals and trying to make as many as possible from scratch. I learned so much from my boss, who encouraged me to think bigger and to constantly seek resources to feed more children. By the time I left, the food ministry was feeding over 200,000 meals a year. It was an incredible experience, and I felt God was preparing me for something else.

While working at the food ministry, I ran into the owner of Wildflowers. She needed help with setup staff, and I was excited to assist. Eventually, I began working part-time at both the food ministry and Wildflowers. Once again, I fell in love with flowers and the creative process. Designing events for brides and organizations was such a joy. One of my first major designs was for the Jazz St. Louis Gala. I researched extensively and thought it would be amazing to use real instruments with flowers as centerpieces. Seeing it come to life was incredible. This began a passion for designing unique events.

Soon, I learned that the owner was selling the business. At first, I doubted my ability to run a business of that size. She had accounts with Jazz St. Louis, the St. Louis Art Museum, and large weddings. It took several months to believe in myself, but my husband encouraged me to take the leap. I stepped out in faith and asked her if I could buy the business. She was excited to sell it to me and stayed on for a year to mentor me. I learned so much from her—not just about designing gorgeous flowers but also about selling events and managing the business.

After purchasing the business, I found myself overwhelmed with details and comparing myself to everyone around me. I had a passion for designing weddings and working with my clients but always felt inadequate in my position. Throughout my career, I've relied on peers, friends, and hired coaches for support and encouragement. Running a business is more than being creative, it is about believing you have been given gifts to use to create beauty in the world to glorify the Creator of all things.

I have had so many amazing experiences in my life. Some hard and many happy and fulfilling. I think each one of them has melded me into who God wants me to be. Our Creator is very intentional about brushing the canvas of our lives. Sometimes we do not always understand why things are happening the way they are but in the words of Mary Engelbright "Bloom where are you planted." I would add…and see how God blossoms you into a gorgeous flower.

Sara Ward is the owner and creative director of Wildflowers Floral Design Studio in St. Louis, Missouri. With a deep appreciation of the beautiful details in nature, she transforms flowers into artful arrangements that inspire and delight. Her passion extends beyond floral design—she is dedicated to helping others discover their purpose by embracing their natural gifts and talents. She believes flowers have the power to connect, heal, and bring joy. Whether designing bespoke arrangements or mentoring others in creative endeavors, Sara's commitment to artistry and purpose shines through. Her work is more than floral design—it's a celebration of nature, creativity, and personal growth.

Please scan the QR code to connect with this author.

Eileen McCaffrey Hedrick with Denise Hedrick Huber

Mission Mentorship

Who mentored you? Who showed you how to live life? Who showed you how to brush your hair and tie your shoes? Most of us were taught by our parents. You become proud when you learn a new skill and see people you love smile. When you see your mom and dad care for someone you begin to mirror their gentle behavior, and you get loving smiles.

I was encouraged in caregiving as it ran in my family tree. My Grandma Mac was a nurse who cared for my grandpa, a Mississippi River Steamboat Captain, and my uncle, a Captain and decorated hero in the Pacific. Even my dad was an award-winning Eagle Scout for saving someone from great injury. I see nurses, priests, sisters, teachers, and homemakers who excelled in their gifts and mentored others to do the same. All doing acts of faith-in-action played out as love through service to others; it's woven in my family tree. My life story has been defined by Mission Mentorship.

Childhood

In the summer of 1942, my parents met when my mom, a USO volunteer, set eyes on a U.S. Coast Guard man. My mother served donuts and hosted tea dances for the U.S. Servicemen after Sunday mass. My father asked her to dance. The next year their wedding dance would begin 60 years of love of God, each other, and family. The following year they welcomed a baby girl and nursed Dad's injury-related discharge back to good health. The next year they headed to New York City for Dad's new job as a radio announcer. There, they waited for a Manhattan baby. . . me! While we lived in New York; we added two brothers for a family of six. Service, compassion, caring, and mentorship would continue to be part of my life.

Early on we watched our parents mentor others. Dad came to New York for radio yet ended up in modeling. Dad began a career he and Mom never imagined. In faith, they committed to modeling until it interfered with their Christian values. Dad ended up becoming one of the top male models of the late 40s and 50s. His resume includes: sailor on the US Bonds, a Texaco Man, many advertisements, smoking cigarettes high up on billboards in Times Square as the Marlboro man. You may have seen his Saturday Evening Post picture, painted by a famous artist, of his handsome Irish face lying in a hammock with his dog after serving his country. He and my mother encouraged and supported young hopefuls in his own agency to lead faith-filled lives while following their dreams. It became normal as they welcomed young people out to our Long Island home for home-style weekends. If we went to church, they went to church. I watched mentorship in action.

I was encouraged to learn new skills, especially when helping others. My Kindergarten report card said, 'Eileen gets her work done well, then goes to help others'. My challenge was allowing my friends to find out what they loved and let them practice getting better. Helping others, made me feel confident in my contributions.

Teenage Life & Service

I enjoyed Mercy High School, and was very involved: student council, cheerleading, service in the "14 Works of Mercy Club", among others. It was here I would meet my future husband, John. I heard his voice freshman year as he rescued a fellow classmate. He said, "Come on guys, leave him alone", while pulling him out of a locker, picking up his books, and asking him if he was, ok? I've been in love with this kind, "knight in shining armor," to this very day.

I grew up serving as a teen and when I began my own family. We washed cars to fundraise, mowed lawns for older people, and brought food to sick neighbors. For two years I cared for an elderly, post-stroke matron a few hours a week. It was in this experience that I knew I could be a nurse, just like my Grandmother and Godmother.

My family listened with fascination, to stories my cousin would tell of her caring for tribes in Africa. When I told her I wanted to come on an African mission trip and serve like her, she told me, 'Take your money and go serve the needy in your own St Louis'. I accepted her wisdom when I chose my vocation and to this day, I continue serving meals to the homeless and allowing God's hand to direct my life.

Nursing Career

While attending St John's Mercy Nursing School, the Sisters of Mercy educated me and my classmates on the health of body, mind, and spirit. They taught us to be compassionate nurses based on a mission of love through service. This mission became foundational to the style of care I would teach others. After graduation, my cousin, Sister Cornelia FSM, and one of the leaders of St Mary's Hospital asked me to work with her team in post-surgery, intensive care. I learned a high level of care, affirmed my vocation in nursing, and continued my education and degree emphasizing Pastoral Care.

In 1968 after John & I were married, we moved to Rolla where I began a nursing position in home care, assessing special-needs children. This experience is where I stood up for the pregnancy of my firstborn, as I was exposed to German measles. I turned down the suggestions to do anything but continue with the hope that everything would work out healthfully. This decision gave us peace of mind because John and I were committed to placing our lives in God's Hands.

John graduated college with a job, moving us to Toledo, Ohio. We met friends, mainly through church that continued to reflect our values. We experienced the joys of parenthood, welcoming a happy, super-active, browned-eyed girl. Two years later, a quieter, happy, strawberry-blond girl arrived. Our little family loved walking through our local woods and trips around Lake Erie. When our oldest was three, we were challenged with her suffering a newly diagnosed case of Juvenile Rheumatoid Arthritis, placing her in the hospital for seven weeks with life-threatening complications. We were mentored and received great encouragement and care from friends and excellent physicians. Quiet family time and saving grace helped our daughter's illness go into remission.

After five years, John received a promotion using his expertise in computers, moving us to Marshalltown, Iowa. We were expecting a baby to arrive, and new friends reached out to help us move and we learned lessons from a small town prayer group. These dear friends, with their gifts of caring and helping each other, enabled us to handle challenges as our new son was born with Spina Bifida. We immediately took on the major challenges of learning what was needed for David to grow and thrive in a world that constantly told us to place him in a facility. Our choice was to go and grow, learn & thrive, helping him strive to be all he was called to be. Miracles happened as we pulled together resources from the Marshalltown Project, specializing in care for children like David. We gratefully met amazing friends who helped us, lifting us above and beyond. I would go to an appointment in Iowa City for David only to have David stay for days. Our prayer group friends would pick up our children from school caring for them until John took over. They prayed for us and fed our spirit and our bellies as they brought us dinners and encouraged us. David's life taught us unconditional love and care for him using home care services with the coordinated efforts of my experiences. David and the staff taught me a lot. I turned and taught my family. Little by little, David played and engaged with his beloved sisters. They lifted his spirits, and he picked up his pace to match the girls.

Three years into David's life, our little miracle daughter was born on St. Nicholas Day. David watched us cuddle her and talk with her, and David picked up the loving ways. He mirrored the actions of her beginnings and began talking with inflection, learned to army crawl around, using the strength of his upper body as he was paralyzed from the waist down. David quickly learned new skills with his little sister encouraging him. When Nicole began walking, David was placed on a standing podium to have him experience standing up on her level and he grabbed toys back with authority and yelled 'mine!' His speech therapist and teachers were amazed as he learned by mimicking Nicole. We in turn taught other parents who had special needs children to do the same. This included how to advocate state Congress for funding in health care and education for special needs children.

We felt blessed with our ability to lead in the special-needs world, yet, our lives drastically changed. David's shunt revision surgery had complications with blockage and sent David into a coma, returning him home to his heavenly Father. Within a week, our lives changed forever as we celebrated David's life at mass. David was now a Saint. It would take years of healing and grieving our feelings of hope we had for his life. David taught us a special kind of love. This would be the basis of our mission ministry mindset going forward.

David died in 1978 and a year later in 1979, John and I were anointed Stephen Ministers. We ministered to those in health crisis', encouraging them in hope. We moved back to St Louis in 1982. I reconnected with Sr. Mary Rocklage at Mercy and a parish friend working in private home care.

They encouraged me to work with them part-time. It felt good being back in bedside nursing and along with being a wife and mother. It completed my feelings of 'giving back' by using my nursing gift, found after the loss of our son, standing up for those who couldn't. I loved being with people in the last stages of their life. I was being prepared.

Martha's Hands Ministry

In 1995, Sr. Rocklage encouraged John and me to develop a Home Care Agency. As I contemplated her suggestions, I went on a retreat and prayed about it. The theme of the retreat was a Mother Theresa quote:

"We serve with our hands, love with our hearts, and seek the face of our creator in those we serve."

That was it! If I was going to start a home care agency, it needed to be built around this mission. This mission ministry drew from all my past experiences of faithful care. When I turned to family and friends for help, they were drawn to Martha's Hands as a care ministry. We were rooted in the wellness care approach of body, mind, and spirit. In 1997, Martha's Hands began with a notepad, a cell phone, and a mission in the basement of my home. With God's blessings, Martha's Hands has provided over six million hours of care to over 9,000 families. Our care ministry mindset has been taught to over 7,000 care team members.

Looking back, we were being prepared by our loving God for our future. We learned God doesn't call the prepared. He prepares the called. Our family began a home care dream where we helped others care for their loved ones. I say to each of you, 'Be Your Own Best Encourager. 'Keep choosing the good! As I mature, I find new gifts that make me happy and fulfilled. They become my passion and gift to share with others. I found myself encouraging others to find their passion and gifts too. Mirroring my mentors, I used the method; watch and listen, learn and do, then turn and teach others to do the same. WWJD

Eileen McCaffrey Hedrick, RN, BSHA is a Co-Founder and Chief of Mission and Nursing of Martha's Hands Home Care Services. Caregiving inspired Eileen throughout her life. Coming from a family of servants (doctors, nurses, priests, and nuns), Eileen studied nursing at St. Johns Mercy Hospital, in partnership with St. Louis University. The Sisters of Mercy mentored her vocation in a nursing. Eileen carried out her vocation while raising four children, including a son with Spina-Bifida. Eileen was rooted in the home care story and turned towards in-home care nursing.

In 1997, she was encouraged to start Martha's Hands; inspired by teachings in compassionate nursing and excellence in body, mind and spirit model. Since then, Eileen has led Martha's Hands beginnings from her basement to becoming one of the largest private duty home care agencies in Missouri. Eileen's Care Ministry has impacted over 9,000 families and trained over 7,000 caregivers.

Eileen mentored Denise Hedrick Huber, her eldest daughter, who grew up caring for her brother, who was born with special needs. This early caregiving experience set her on a path to make a positive difference in other people's lives. Sharing a mutual passion, she co-founded Martha's Hands Home Care Services with her mother in 1997. Denise leads their inspiring efforts in Marketing, Community relations, recruitment and employee engagement. She is your tour guide for living well and aging successfully.

Please scan the QR code to connect with this author.

Marianne Biangardi

The Ripple of Kindness: Mentoring Through Love

A legacy is not necessarily about what you leave behind, but more about how you lift others up along the way. My mom's legacy is one of love and kindness. When visiting her home, my niece Bella once said, "This house smells like old people and kindness." Everyone loves my mom, and it's because of who she is and how she makes you feel. My other niece Livi says, "Grandma is my most prized possession," and all the grandkids agree.

My mom's acts of kindness are part of the framework of her everyday life. I remember growing up, she was always looking out for others. "Can one of you kids run a plate of food over to Lorraine? I have some extra food from dinner, and I know she would enjoy it." She was always helping our elderly neighbors, and as Lorraine got older, my mom would bring her newspaper up to the door and start her morning coffee. Her love language must be acts of service—whether it was making meals or running errands, my mom was always thinking of others. She encouraged us to do the same. Help a neighbor, bring a plate of food, visit with older folks. It was her way of teaching us that service to others is an essential part of life.

My mom's core concepts of mentorship and lifting others up is her true legacy. She mentored us with her wisdom. As a child, if I wasn't sure how to finish a school project or start a research paper, my mom wouldn't always give me the answer. Instead, she'd say, "Well, have you thought about it like this?" She would guide me to think in a new way, offering perspective rather than direct answers. She was always encouraging me to find my own path. This mentorship didn't stop when I grew up. Even now, as a mom myself, when I face challenges, my mom doesn't give me the solution; she offers resources or suggestions, like a link to a Focus on the Family podcast. She taught us not just to be kind, but to actively support others.

My mom's words on happiness resonate deeply with me: "Perfect happiness isn't possible in life, but there are things you can do to be a happy person. It's the little things you do every day that make you special. Each day you have opportunities to make good choices—try not to miss them." These words shaped my approach to life, and now, I try to pass them along to my own kids.

My goal, just like my mom's, is to lift others up. Her legacy has caused a ripple effect in my life. When I meet new people in my network, I encourage them to join our circle. I help our neighbors and mentor my kids in the same way. Whether it's helping elderly neighbors shovel snow or sharing extra cookies, I encourage my children to think about others and find ways to support them. My kids, Zoey, Claire, and Ronin, now ask how they can help too. They volunteer at the food bank and help neighbors. These small acts of service are already becoming part of their lives, just as they were for me.

Zoey and Claire love spending time with Grandma—whether it's learning to cook or doing homework together. They admire her patience and kindness. Grandma has become a steady presence in their lives, teaching them life's most important lessons. Ronin, too, has taken after Grandma, always wanting to check on our elderly neighbor, Marie, just as Grandma checks in on others. These little moments of mentorship from my mom are already shaping how my kids view the world and how they show kindness to those around them.

Mentorship, for me, isn't just about giving advice; it's about creating relationships. I've learned that we need a variety of mentors in our lives. My friend Rachel recently told me that we should have up to seven mentors, but I believe I have even more, especially when you factor in peer-to-peer and reverse mentoring. I can spot an authentic person quickly and bring them into my circle. Many of my closest friends and peer mentors started as work relationships. I met my best friend Maria at the Old Country Buffet during high school. Now, thirty years later we are still working together. We are both marketing managers, still each other's most trusted advisors. My circle is filled with people who have the same characteristics as my mom: kindness, simplicity, gratitude, and generosity. They affect how I interact with others and how I mentor, just as my mom did for me.

The relationships I've built all stem from my mom's teachings about the importance of lifting others up. I believe that good people always find each other. Mentorship isn't just about offering advice; it's about forming lifelong connections and sharing values. I love helping others find their own path, just as my mom helped me. Kindness, gratitude, and trust are some of the most important qualities my mom showed me as a mentor. She taught us to look out for those who need extra encouragement, whether it's offering a compliment, making a call to someone you haven't talked to in a while, or volunteering your time.

One of the most powerful lessons my mom gave me was the way she lived. She was always helping others—not through grand gestures, but with small, consistent acts of kindness. I remember a time when one of the elderly women in our neighborhood had just undergone chemotherapy and needed help lifting a gift into her car for her son. I was busy with errands, but without hesitation, I helped her. It only took a few minutes, but it was something my mom would have done.

Trusting in God is a central part of my mom's life, and it's something she passed on to me. Faith played a huge role when my daughter Claire was diagnosed with a life-threatening illness called HLH, and it was our trust in God that helped us navigate the challenging times. My mom's faith, love, and support were essential in guiding us through. Our faith continues to guide us, and it was our neighbors and friends who showed up to help us when we needed it most. I can never repay them, but I try to pay it forward by helping others. I'm reminded of the quote by John Bunyan: "You have not lived today until you have done something for someone who can never repay you." This is the essence of mentorship and the ripple effect of kindness.

My mom's lessons helped me grow as a person. Her unwavering faith that everything would work out is something I've adopted in my own life. Sometimes doors close, and it's not always the outcome you wanted, but trusting that God has different plans has shaped how I approach life. I didn't know where my art degree would take me, but it led me to a fulfilling career in marketing at an accounting firm. My mom's unconditional support and love were all I needed. She never questioned my career choices; she trusted me.

Every day, I meet people I can help. Every day, I try to live simply and be grateful for what I have. My mom's influence shows up in how I mentor others. She taught me that when you meet someone you admire, you should try to model the trait you admire. My mom is a great listener, shares wisdom, and cares about others. She believes we are all here for a reason and that God wants to use us. If you see someone who needs help—whether it's with finding a new job or needing a new friend—they might need you to show up.

I also make a point to connect with people in my professional network, regardless of what I might gain from the meeting. I believe in helping people without expecting anything in return. It's not about mutual benefit—it's about showing kindness. In mentoring the next generation, both my kids and the people in my network, I try to explain that the key to building authentic relationships is giving. If you give, you will receive in ways you can't imagine. I'm honored to have a lasting impact on those I mentor, just as my mom did for me.

Thank you, Mom, for teaching me your values and leaving a legacy of mentorship, kindness, and service. Your legacy continues to live on through me and my family. You've shown us that the smallest acts of kindness can make the biggest difference. I am committed to living a life of service, kindness, and gratitude, and to passing these lessons on to the next generation. Just as you have done for me, I will continue to mentor and lift others up, creating a ripple effect of kindness that will last for years to come.

Senior Associate, Marketing & Business Development, UHY Advisors

Marianne Biangardi specializes in brand visibility, lead generation, client relations, and marketing. Marianne was named one of the "Top 100 People to Know to Succeed in Business" by the St. Louis SBM. Marianne is involved in several industry organizations, including the American Subcontractors Association Midwest Council, SITE Improvement, The Association of General Contractors, St. Louis Construction Consumers Council, The National Tool Manufacturing Association, and is a co-founder of *Made in Missouri.*

Outside of her professional life, Marianne has been happily married to her husband, Matt, for over 20 years, and they share three children—Zoey, Claire, and Ronin. She enjoys fitness, walking, and unwinding with podcasts. She's an avid sports fan, with a particular love for the St. Louis Blues and the Kansas City Chiefs. At home, she enjoys spending time with her two cats and her German Shepherd.

Marianne is committed to leaving a lasting impact, both professionally and personally, through the meaningful connections she builds and the legacy of kindness and service she strives to live out every day.

Please scan the QR code to connect with this author.

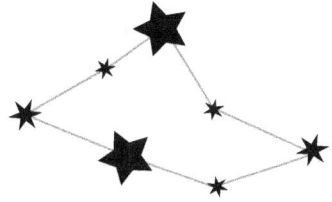

Gretchen Kingma

Permission To...

Giving others *genuine permission* to push the limits and think outside the box is the greatest gift we can give. My mentors have been there to help me push the status quo.

It was a bright summer day in 2013 when I, along with another Occupational Therapy (OT) student and two of our professors, piled into a university-issued van for the long drive back to Saint Louis, MO, from Moore, OK. We had spent days immersed in tornado cleanup, working alongside people who had lost everything and exploring the critical role of OT in natural disaster recovery. As the journey wound down, Dr. Sherry Muir, one of our professors, reflected on our efforts and simply said, "Really, OTs can do anything." Her words resonated deeply and have stayed with me ever since, shaping my belief in the limitless potential of our profession.

The very situation we found ourselves in was a living example that Dr. Muir's words were true. I was a Level 2 fieldwork student with Dr. Jeanne Eichler and my objective was to build and implement an eight-week program for college and career-bound teens on the autism spectrum. One day I was teaching thirteen-to-fifteen-year-old girls how to properly shave their legs (sounds weird, but definitely a necessary skill for a college-bound teen, right!?), and the next, I was picking up rubble in a tornado-stricken town.

To this day, I am deeply grateful that Dr. Muir and Dr. Eichler proposed pausing the Autism Speaks program for a few days to make the journey to Oklahoma. Their leadership during this experience gave me the permission to problem-solve, adapt, and dream bigger than I ever thought possible.

It's the same kind of permission I was given by Ms. Kim Cowan back in high school at Cor Jesu Academy. I vividly remember a day when our class was discussing a poem. While all my classmates seemed to interpret it the same way, my perspective was completely different—not just slightly off, but wildly divergent. When I shared my thoughts, I was met with audible laughs from the room. Thankfully, Ms. Cowan stepped in immediately, shutting down the mockery and turning it into a teachable moment. She reminded us that poetry, like so many things in life, isn't about being right or wrong—it's about seeing things differently and embracing unique perspectives.

I'll always be grateful for the permission she gave me to think differently.

I carried that lesson with me into my first occupational therapy role at SSM Rehabilitation Hospital, where I was fortunate to work alongside an incredible group of peer mentors. A heartfelt shoutout to Andie, Christie, Ashley, Rachel, Kathleen, and Lisa—the talented OTs who supported and guided me during those early days of my career. Their mentorship and camaraderie were invaluable, and I couldn't have asked for a better team to learn from.

During this time, I was tasked with covering another OT's maternity leave, which meant stepping into one of the most challenging settings in the hospital: the brain injury unit. As a new graduate, I was understandably terrified to work with such unpredictable patients. The set-up of the open gym where we treated our patients became my safe haven, allowing me to collaborate and lean on my peers for support during therapy sessions. It was there that I learned to face my fears, rely on teamwork, and grow as a clinician.

One patient who will always stay with me was a young woman, "M," who had suffered a traumatic brain injury in a motor vehicle accident. When she joined my caseload, her Glasgow Coma Scale score was alarmingly low (a clinical tool used to assess a person's level of consciousness after a brain injury, ranging from 3 to 15, with lower scores indicating more severe impairment), indicating she was minimally responsive. During a family interview, I discovered that M shared my love of duck hunting—a connection that sparked an idea. The patient-focused and creative treatment sessions I had observed from my peers gave me the permission to think outside the box when working with M. Together, we used the action of shouldering a shotgun at the edge of a therapy mat to improve her core strength, balance, and endurance. We even incorporated an actual duck call to help build her breath control and lung capacity. That experience not only gave me the permission to be creative but also reinforced its transformative power—a lesson that has shaped my career ever since.

After spending several years at the rehab hospital, I made the switch to senior living—a decision that brought me to my absolute favorite population. I've always LOVED working with older adults, and my time at The Gatesworth was nothing short of extraordinary. While interdisciplinary team meetings often came with their challenges (especially when families were involved), I had the privilege of working under an exceptional therapy manager, Lynn Lyon. Lynn consistently led by example, unwaveringly advocating for what was in the absolute best interest of the patient—no one else. Her compassion and determination to prioritize the most vulnerable in the room inspired me deeply. She gave me permission to fully embrace the calling to serve others, no matter what role I find myself in.

When meeting new people or presenting to an audience, I often feel the need to over-explain or justify my transition from healthcare to real estate. But the truth is, thanks to the encouragement of impactful colleagues along the way, I've built a career and business that makes me excited to jump out of bed every morning.

Today, as I enter my 8th year in the real estate business, I'm proud to say I've not only quadrupled my clinical income but also amplified my impact. To date, I have had the privilege of serving over 250 families with their housing needs, mentored 6 occupational therapy students who want to do similar work, and have partnered with another amazing OT, Tiffany Dill, to start an additional company doing accessibility consulting. I'm incredibly grateful for the guidance of real estate leaders and coaches like Russ Nolting, Katie Force White, and Erin Joy. Their mentorship has given me the permission to be unapologetically bold in business and to pursue my vision with relentless determination.

Without the mentorship of these incredible women, I would never have found the courage to make a bold career pivot in 2017. Leaving clinical occupational therapy—especially with six figures of graduate school debt—might have seemed crazy to most people (and, honestly, to me too). Deep down, I knew that by combining my OT expertise with a career in real estate, I could truly transform how people view and experience aging in their homes. It wasn't just a career change; it was an opportunity to make a meaningful impact in a whole new way.

The mentors in my life taught me to push the status quo. Without the permission to dream big, to think differently, to be creative, to serve, and to be bold, there is no chance I would have been able to achieve what I have today. I vow to take these lessons and forever instill them in my kids and anyone I have the opportunity to work alongside in the future.

Gretchen Kingma is a highly accomplished REALTOR and occupational therapist ranked among the Top 100 Keller Williams agents in her five-state region. With credentials in accessibility and aging-in-place (OTR/L, CAPS, ECHM), she specializes in creating thoughtful housing solutions for clients as well as training other REALTORS and entrepreneurs to build personal brands online.

Her expertise has been featured in the AOTA Practice Journal, and she has authored and delivered a state-approved 3-hour curriculum for the Missouri Real Estate Commission. Passionate about merging healthcare and real estate, Gretchen has helped over 300 families achieve their housing goals and continues to mentor others in the industry.

Please scan the QR code to connect with this author.

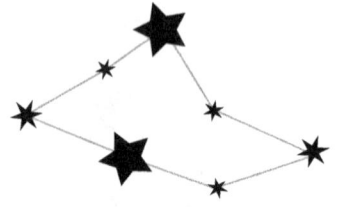

Kate Manfull

The Art of Leading with Laughter

They want my hat.

They giggle and chase me through the house. They must get my hat. I leap over the couch and roll through the living room like a clumsy ninja - gasp, I'm trapped! They attack me with their laughter and sticky, freezie-pop fingers, swiping the flowered underwear from my head. "That was not a hat," they declare in victory through their laughter.

I'd been sitting there for a few minutes prior folding laundry wearing my daughter's tiny underwear on my head. They were a little tight, if I recall, but well worth the chase and belly laughs that followed.

I love to laugh, but even more so, I love to make others laugh.

Using humor to connect, bring joy, and offer levity is how I navigate life. Humor, when used at the right moment, can draw people closer, break the ice, and add perspective. It can change the conversation, diffuse, distract, and make way for better and brighter solutions. It's being vulnerable in a way that allows everyone around you to enter in with more ease. It's with humor that I lead our home, my relationships, and my creative agency.

Vulnerability

The foundation of my business was built in the wee hours of the night freelancing graphic design so I could play all day with our little ones. The laughter and joy provided the relief I needed to run the double shift. Call it crazy or call it completely insane, either way, you're right. I loved every minute of it as a creator and a mom.

The kitchen dance parties, fake cooking shows, costumes, and music-filled days fed my creative soul in ways that I never could have imagined. It made me a better artist and a more patient, empathic friend, mom, and leader.

In our work and in our play, we can draw from that ability to show up unapologetically as ourselves. That vulnerability creates space for empathy. It allows for everything from unpolished questions and diversity of perspective to improved listening and even those bad ideas to come through. It was like that time I agreed "The world is your canvas" and the kids ended up drawing all over their bedroom walls.

It's with this approach I can level out the stress of running a creative agency and an active household of teens without losing myself in the process. I gave permission to laugh at myself. That's what's funny about leading with humor. It's not about being funny at all. It's about not taking ourselves too seriously.

It breaks down barriers to make way for deeper connection by being vulnerable. In doing so, I'm making way for the hard conversations, the serious decisions, and the emotionally charged moments to also take up the space they require.

What I'm offering is an approach that allows you to live lighter. This is a way to cut unnecessary stress and find more happiness. It's about ultimately pouring that positivity into the world and watching it all come back tenfold.

Empowerment.

Agency life can be stressful. Client demands, competitive co-workers, unreasonable expectations, and impossible time restraints can cause burnout and retention issues. Amazing creative people have spun out under these circumstances.

When I started Fierce Creative Agency, I wanted to do things differently.

I had been working nights as a graphic designer in those years before the kids went to school. I had clients all over the country that didn't care where I was, if I had kids, or a llama in the backyard. They wanted the work back by the next day and I delivered. In the same vein, my meeting time was unavailable for clients as I was already booked—at the zoo, the park, or in the living room fort.

When it was time to decide if I was going to continue working from home or give this agency-life thing a go, I went all in. Fierce Creative is a boutique agency offering consistent and cohesive brand representation for its clients. We offer brand design, website design and development, and content marketing ranging from social media and email marketing to experiential and paid digital ad strategy.

In the beginning, it was just the two of us. I brought on my first intern full-time. She became one of my most trusted business partners and now, ten years later, is a leading web designer and developer working part-time for me while raising her own two little ones at home. It's a true joy to offer her a way to stay active in her career and be the mom she wants to be. It's a story I know well.

Designing a life and creating an agency that worked for all of us was my focus. We've always had shorter workdays (so I could be at the bus stop at both ends of my day), two remote workdays each week (for deep dive and flexibility), and unlimited vacation time. I trust the team to get their work done. We take care of each other and deliver for our clients.

The team I have shares my entrepreneurial spirit and my over-achieving drive for success. They also have an undying desire to create something meaningful. We feed off of creative collaboration. They also like to laugh.

We've built a culture around laughing through stress. We allow ourselves to share and address the pressure but also release unnecessary stress. An example was the time an intern accidentally ordered 2,500 pens with their name and phone number on them, or the 200 mailers that were returned because we didn't tape them properly. We also do push-ups if a spelling mistake makes it to the client. It only seems fair.

My role at Fierce has changed as the agency has grown, but it's clear that while I am a mentor to my team, they are mentoring me into a better leader every day. When we are inspired, motivated, and challenged in our work, we turn out even greater results for each other and our clients.

I'm acutely aware that I am an instrumental piece of their career journey. I never take that lightly even as I'm bebopping around the office. I want them to feel seen, heard, and appreciated for their individualism. They are empowered to try new things, make mistakes, speak up and succeed. I truly believe I'm in their lives for a specific purpose and am charged by the thrill of discovering what that is for each of them.

I ask about their bigger goals and dreams beyond Fierce. I want to pour into where they want to go, not just fill the immediate need. It's empowering to have someone believe in you. I know.

I have been forever changed by the countless women who have influenced my journey from the boss at my internship in Washington D.C. and my first corporate job in St. Louis where my superior advised me to get agency experience, to those early days of mom life and to the women who

I look up to today as partners and clients. Having others see your potential makes you feel that you can do anything.

My team can do anything. It's in our monthly one-on-one meetings we measure progress toward their goals and how I can aid them in that journey. We had a writer on our team who had desired to be a college professor. Any education-based clients we had, became hers to manage. When she came to me with an offer to become an adjunct professor, I was elated. It's what we had planned for. We adjusted her schedule so she can do both - work at Fierce and lead a classroom. Next, she desires to publish her own book. You can guarantee I'm working on that with her as well.

One teammate wanted to speak at conferences. When he found an opportunity, we made space and showed up to support him. He crushed it and we can't wait for the next one. Another wanted to learn motion design and 3D modeling and we created capacity for him to explore and play. Another is an amazing artist and anytime we can offer her outlets from office window displays to illustration projects, we do. When the team was feeling a need to "create for the sake of creating" without ties to client work, we made our own ezine to showcase their talents.

I am inspired when I see them in their element - competing in horse shows, shining in weight-lifting competitions, completing house-flipping projects, or performing music at Renaissance fairs. There's simply no downside to mentoring and supporting, lifting and caring for others' dreams, especially as they show up each day to support one of mine.

Inspiration

We can't stop there. Fierce Creative has also become the team that supports and encourages the next generation of creatives. We are mentors to each other and those who come next. There are far too many creative minds that are told there's no money, no future, no use for entering the arts and communications industry.

We beg to differ. What we do is essential to all industries, to all people, everywhere. To share our passion for this work with the next generation of creatives, we open our doors to job shadows, tours, internships, round table discussions, career counseling, mock interviews, and portfolio reviews.

Each summer I stand before hundreds of students at Media Now, a summer camp my husband and I designed to level up high school journalism students and their programs. Within minutes of meeting our students, I have them on stage dipping their faces in plates of cool whip, chasing each other on scooters for a relay, and parading around in outfits made of toilet paper. Why do they do it? Why do they volunteer to jump up on stage and risk looking a little, dare we say…foolish? Because I've already leveled the playing field.

I've already worn the oversized pink sunglasses while reading the rules, eaten the Oreo dipped in hot sauce, and challenged someone to a handstand competition for no apparent reason. I've already looked *more* foolish. The walls are down. The space has been made ready. Students can show up more authentically. They're primed for connection and growth.

Thousands of students have gone through this program over the 15 years since it began. These talents have gone on to work as broadcasters, sports marketers, community news reporters, writers, animators, and marketers, but also as doctors, educators, community leaders, engineers, and activists.

The Fierce Creative team serves as the fuel behind Media Now's year-round support that culminates with a week of intense fun each summer. It's our way of giving back and paying it forward.

The *Be You. Be Fierce.* mantra at Fierce is not just hanging on our office walls, but it's how we show up in the world - authentically, unapologetically. We encourage these young students to step out and step up. We show the next generation a pathway to discovering their own strengths, all while strengthening ours.

The Truth About Laughter

Laughter feels good. Positive energy is contagious. When we show vulnerability in the smaller moments, it allows us to dive deeper when it really matters. When the stakes are higher, the risk greater, the challenge wider, that's when the groundwork of leading with humor, vulnerability, and empathy shows its true colors.

It's the humor and silliness of the smallest moments that open the door to long-standing relationships and lasting connection. That's when the real change happens. It's where the good stuff bubbles to the top. It's where discomfort guides us and pushes us to be better friends, parents, co-workers, community members, neighbors, mentors, and human beings.

Each night, all I really want to have accomplished is to have made someone's day a little better. The measurement? A smile, a wink, a nod, a look, or a shared laugh. The entry fee is low, my friends. The benefits are high. Perhaps all we need to get started is to find the right hat.

Kate Manfull, founder of Fierce Creative Agency, is a visual communicator who brings fresh storytelling techniques and creative solutions through visual content to help brands across digital and physical spaces. She built her career as a visual communicator in corporate advertising, at a video production house, and with a public relations agency prior to founding Fierce. The creative powerhouse serves up all aspects of brand appearances from design and website development to content marketing, live event coverage, and paid digital ad strategies.

She is the director of Media Now and holds degrees from Webster University and Truman State University. She is a performer at heart, and full of risk-taking, entrepreneurial spirit. Kate actively works to create more inclusive and equitable spaces through her work and relationships.

She gives a shoutout to her circle for supporting her wild ideas and sharing in the laughter, her husband for believing in her, her parents for instilling unwavering confidence, and her two creatively talented kids whose presence encourages her to continue showing up authentically and unapologetically every day. Be you. Be Fierce.

Please scan the QR code to connect with this author.

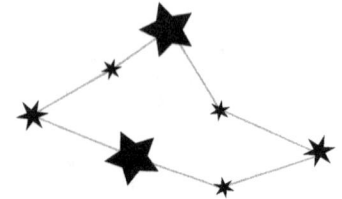

Amanda Bradham-Little

Okay, You WILL Be:
Find Your Yoda

A long time ago (six years), in a galaxy far, far away (St. Louis, MO)… life as I knew it had ended. Like Luke Skywalker stepping into uncharted territory, not knowing what battles lay ahead, I was receiving life-changing news. Little did I know I would meet my own Yoda to help guide my path. On May 30, 2019, I had just left a job I loved. I was exhausted but ready for a new, perhaps calmer, challenge. Even now, it almost hurts too much to relive the beginning. It feels like self-preservation to avoid those feelings of fear and anxiety. The mental and physical pain of those first two years seems like a lifetime ago. I assume it's like childbirth—so excruciating that every mother swears she'll never do it again, yet somehow, the pain fades.

I woke up blind in my left eye the day before I started at Pace Properties. That was a real doozy. Riding in my new boss's convertible to lunch with the top down like we were flying down the German Autobahn was even more interesting. I must have failed at every conversation I tried to participate in. What was happening? Was this stress? Just one week earlier, we had said goodbye to our beloved fur baby on Mother's Day. I was going from working more than sixty hours a week with a team of people I loved like family, to an entirely new industry full of strangers.

The eye doctor that day was oh-so casual when he mentioned I likely had optic neuritis and it was "probably Multiple Sclerosis." He said that's how it's often first diagnosed. I had no clue what Multiple Sclerosis (MS) even was. I immediately pictured the Jerry Lewis telethon. Eight long days followed, filled with tears, countless frantic appointments with Dr. Google (which made everything worse), referrals to neuro-ophthalmologists who had availability in August, and my own relentless push for bloodwork and an MRI. Then, one morning, I woke to numb fingertips that felt like they were coated in superglue. The next day, I felt a crushing tightness wrapped around my left arm. It was like boa constrictors coiling around me.

Really? It had to be snakes? If you knew my mischievous older brother and my childhood, you'd understand why that's my worst fear. The sensation was a mix of numbness and suffocating tightness, and no matter how I tried to explain it, words never seemed enough. That's the thing about MS—its symptoms are indescribable, yet undeniable.

I begged to move my MRI up. Lying in that tube with a cage covering my head like Hannibal Lecter, tears streamed down my face. My body was still, but my mind ran a full-on marathon. I knew in my soul it wasn't good news. I was barely dressed when the tech handed me a cordless phone and led me to a cold, sterile room. On the other end was my doctor. "I'm so sorry," he said. "Your MRI confirms it. You have Multiple Sclerosis." Ironically, I later learned that day that it was World MS Day.

The months that followed were agony—physically, mentally, emotionally. Did the physical pain cause the mental anguish, or did the mental turmoil cause the physical symptoms? The answer to both was yes. I was trapped in a cycle of torment. I couldn't be alone. I couldn't sleep. I sometimes drove to work at 4:00 a.m. or 5:00 a.m. just to try and rest in a quiet corner of the parking garage. I tried to keep up appearances, to pretend I was okay. I wasn't. Was this my new normal? Could I live with this level of pain forever? Did I have a choice? It was as if I was walking through fire. The world couldn't see the fatigue, the pain, the fog that clouded my mind. MS is called an invisible illness for a reason. To the world, I looked fine, but inside, the fire raged on. I was burning from the inside out, but no one could see the flames.

As the days ticked by, the number of amazing people who came into my life ticked up. There are a few people I credit for my survival. My husband Jason, of course, and by what I can only describe as a God Wink, there was Dr. Barry Singer, the Director of the MS Center for Innovations in Care at Missouri Baptist Medical Center, who became my MS neurologist and just so happened to be on call that day at the hospital.

Perhaps the most unexpected, yet invaluable, support came from a stranger named Jon Franko. Jon lives with MS and was introduced to me by a friend. He became what I call my MS Yoda (you might call him a mentor) who took every call I made, no matter the time of day and no matter what he was doing. We were able to connect a couple of weeks after I was diagnosed and I was beginning to feel the weight of the emotional toll MS was taking on me. He provided a safe space where I could unpack my fear, grief, and uncertainty, helping me make sense of the emotional chaos that often followed the physical challenges.

At one of my lowest points, when I felt like I was drowning in fear, I texted Jon. I explained that I felt like I was going backward. I felt as bad as I did at the beginning. I felt hopeless like this would never get better. I was not in good shape. I felt like I was in crisis mode. I just wanted the pain to go away.

His response was, "Takes time, grasshopper. "I promise. It gets better. You're in the woods right now, so you can't see it. But trust me, better days are ahead."

When I replied, telling him I hoped he was right and admitting I didn't remember ever feeling that low in my life, he responded, "Yup. I've been there. Totally get it. It's all fear right now. Keep that in mind. Nothing has happened yet that's bad. You lost some vision. And it's back! You're already winning. Seriously. That alone should give you comfort. You get another attack again; you simply win again. You haven't seen it yet, and won't for a bit, but you've been given a gift with this diagnosis. Trust me."

I thought he was crazy. A gift? Not in this lifetime. That actually made me angrier than receiving the diagnosis. Nothing about this felt like a gift.

There was a time in this process when I was convinced I was having a relapse. I stormed into my neurologist's office. I had no appointment and gave him no warning; only to realize the "symptom" was the tag on my dress grazing my thigh. I might have been their craziest patient. (Still might be.)

Then, in October 2019, Leo entered my life. He was our new Shih Tzu pup, my tiny lifeline. Potty training was a nightmare, but it was also salvation. Rain, snow, sun, wind—it didn't matter. I walked him through our yard like an FBI agent on a grid search. I needed the distraction. I needed not to think about MS, even for a moment. I honestly wasn't sure if I would ever become *me* again. I cried more than I thought humanly possible.

One day, during my darkest moment, I told Jason I wasn't sure I could keep going. As soon as the words left my mouth, I knew they weren't what I truly meant. I didn't want to give up, I just couldn't stand feeling this way anymore. While walking Leo, my thoughts turned to the worst-case scenario. It felt like I was reaching for control, but I couldn't escape the hamster wheel of anxiety and fear. I was stuck in a constant state of fight or flight.

Patients with MS are more than twice as likely as the general population to attempt suicide and almost twice as likely to take their lives. I refused to be part of that statistic. More times than I thought about giving up, I whispered to myself, "I will get through this. *I WILL get through this.*"

Here's the truth: We're all going to have something. We're all going to walk through fire. For some, it's the loss of a loved one. For others, it's cancer. For me, it's MS, but we don't get to choose the fire. We only get to choose *how* we walk through it.

I don't pretend to be the bravest person out there. I don't claim my struggle is the hardest or my pain the worst. I do know this: I made a choice. A choice to turn my pain into purpose. To fight for a cure. To be a voice for hope.

During one of my many panic attacks, I stumbled upon a quote from Brene Brown: "One day, you'll tell your story of how you overcame what you're going through now, and it will become part of someone else's survival guide."

I made a promise to myself that I would live that quote. If you're walking through fire right now, hear me: **Okay, you WILL be.** Share your story. Let someone with a bucket help. Find your Yoda. The "Yodas" have been through it. They can guide you when you can't see the way. Don't keep your hell a secret. Secrets don't get cures. Secrets don't find hope. Hope is what saves us.

Yoda was right. It turns out MS is a gift.

Amanda is the Vice President of Marketing and Community Relations and oversees marketing and branding with Pace Properties and the St. Louis office of Avison Young. With 25 years of experience in marketing, events, and promotion, she has won numerous awards, including Philanthropist of the Year, twice awarded Mentor of the Year, and the National Multiple Sclerosis Society's 2024 Person of Courage. Determined not to sit on the sidelines of illness after her diagnoses, Amanda became involved with the National MS Society by joining her local chapter's Walk MS committee and forming a Walk team. In October 2020, she joined the National MS Society Board of Trustees. In 2022, she and two dear friends (Tori and Stephanie) started a fundraiser named Paws for a Cause, Because MS Needs a Dog-gone Cure. To date, Amanda has raised over $300,000 for the National MS Society. She also credits her mom, Sharon, best friends Shanyon and Laura, and husband Jason—her knight in shining armor—as heroes in overcoming her diagnosis.

Please scan the QR code to connect with this author.

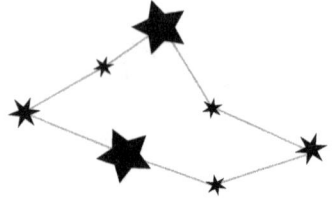

Rhonda Travers

Creating Impact

Do you remember as a kid when you had to run and do sprints in gym class?

I hated that. I would have laughed in disbelief if you told me I would become hooked on 5k races as an adult. I walked my first 5k in 2014. I was drawn to anticipation and excitement with all the participants and my friends before the race started. I also loved crossing the finish line, collecting the medals, and gathering swag at the end of each race. Later, I started training with others to improve my personal record. I learned how to build endurance to jog and walk in intervals. I went from a 20-minute mile to a 13-minute mile. I signed up for a race to maintain the intervals throughout the entire race. This was a stretch. My pace leader kept encouraging me, even though I was the last one in the group. One fellow member aligned her pace with mine to cross that finish line and celebrate together. During this time, I had the opportunity to start a women's social walk group where I was able to share my passion for walking. I would hear comments change from "I can't do a 5k" to "I can't believe we just walked 3 miles!".

Leadership is like a 5k race. After the countdown, some dash out fast, ready to take the lead. They have trained for this moment and have a goal, such as exceeding their personal record. Others are talking, walking, and laughing with their friends. By mile 1, they have their cadence. They may be following others ahead of them and are inspired to keep up the pace. They may be talking to their race partner and giving words of encouragement to keep going. Then there is the adrenaline of crossing the finish line, getting that medal, and celebrating with others.

I probably would not have completed numerous 5k races if I had not surrounded myself with friends who enjoyed walking and who encouraged each other to achieve their personal best. When you have others in your life to guide you, inspire you, prompt you, and celebrate you, this is your circle of influence. This is why Jim Rohn's quote, "You are the average of the five people you surround yourself with," is one of my favorites.

If you had told me as an Accounting Major studying for the CPA exam that I would lead others during a 30-year corporate career and then pursue my dream to become a business consultant, leadership development trainer, professional speaker, and author, I would have also laughed in disbelief.

My circle of influence, those I surrounded myself with both intentionally and unintentionally, has a significant impact on my journey. I am grateful for the following women who changed the trajectory of *four critical parts of my journey*.

In high school, I took my first accounting class in my junior year and loved it. In my senior year, I had a conflict when Acapella Choir was offered at the same time as Accounting 2. I enjoyed both. I shared my concern with my accounting teacher, and she was willing to meet with me during my free hour so I could complete the class. She created this option because she recognized my passion and curiosity for accounting. Because of her guidance and mentorship, I knew I wanted to complete my accounting degree and CPA certification before I even started college.

During college, my Business Writing professor observed how I led my group project when one of our members couldn't attend the final presentation after weeks of preparation. I naturally jumped in and presented her portion without hesitation. My professor recognized my leadership and offered an opportunity to be her office assistant, where I helped with documenting processes. As my curiosity for the learning environment grew, she expanded my role to tutor a few students. I soon discovered another passion – training and educating others.

During my corporate career, I continued pursuing my passion for coaching and training others in various managerial roles. Like crossing that finish line, it was an adrenaline rush to see a light bulb go off while facilitating a training session or celebrating an employee promotion after coaching them.

After 20 years with one employer, I again sought guidance, now from a career coach, to explore other opportunities for growth within a different industry while leveraging my internal audit expertise. Her first question that resonated with me was what I would do if money wasn't an object. My answer was to launch my own training and consulting company. Her guidance prompted me to visualize I would someday pursue this dream to further align my passion and purpose.

Four years later, in 2019, I joined a networking group of high-achieving women, ***Little Black Book: Women in Business***, where I started disclosing this dream. Many women shared their personal journey of leaving a corporate career to pursue their dreams. This was so inspiring to me. These women also nudged me and asked me why I was waiting. They saw what made me light up and shine and encouraged me to turn my dream into a reality now instead of "someday". I soon launched my business in 2021. Those who will *lift* you up become the power of your circle of influence.

Just as runners dash from the starting line with the goal of exceeding their personal record or placing first, I would not be able to lead unless I also had clarity around an end goal. This would be my legacy. One of my favorite quotes from Maya Angelou is "People will forget what you said, people will forget what you did, but people will never forget how you made them feel." My goal is to create a positive impact by adding value, creating transformation, and empowering others. This is the *legacy* that I want to leave.

Newly promoted managers often focus on the activities that worked as individual contributors. Often communication is centered around what employees need to do for "my deadline" and to further "my career". As a leader, creating a positive impact has a mindset that is bigger than yourself. It is a "we" mindset and not a "me" mindset. How are "we" moving together to achieve our deadline that impacts the company? How can we celebrate successes as a team?

In my corporate leadership roles, it has been a privilege to work with hundreds of professionals. It wasn't about getting tasks done because I said so as a manager. It was about having employees understand and own their role and their impact in the company. Just like my two mentors in high school and college, I also spent time understanding what motivated them and how I could help them with their career goals.

As a business owner, I leverage my background and create a bigger impact by helping multiple organizations create success for their employees. I share my philosophy that people need tools, training, and support to be effective. All employees should be comfortable asking questions, have a platform to be heard, and be empowered to understand and own their roles. Leadership is about creating a collaborative environment where people can thrive.

Personally, I also pursued volunteer leadership roles to create a positive impact in the community. I love guiding a team toward a goal, such as fundraising, membership engagement, and board direction. It has been an honor to be involved with organizations, such as the Girl Scouts, to create a positive impact on future female leaders.

My goal in sharing my journey as an author is to broaden my impact on empowering others. My intention, my legacy, is for one piece of my story to resonate that will inspire and nudge you to achieve your goal. When you focus on creating success for others, you can create your own legacy where abundance and fulfillment are returned to you.

Although I intentionally pursued leadership roles both personally and professionally throughout my journey, you don't need "Manager" or "President" in your title. We are all leaders in our lives. Your actions and words are creating an impact, even if you aren't aware of what that impact is.

For example, I often meet with other women with the intention of learning each other's businesses and how we can support each other by creating connections. What has unexpectedly resonated with many was not what I do, but my personal journey of aligning my purpose and passion.

Within this past year, I received a high compliment that I was someone's mentor. I didn't even know it. We connected after I provided a webinar and started meeting for lunch every month where we shared stories, brainstormed ideas, and had great conversations. Later, she told me I was her mentor. Words I shared lifted her with where she was on her journey. This truly fills my heart. That has a positive impact. That is a legacy.

No matter where you are in your 5k journey, learn from those guiding the way in front of you, pace yourself with those who will celebrate you, and know there are others behind you who are being inspired by your journey. How will *you* leave a legacy that will lead, lift, and create a positive impact for others?

Rhonda Travers fulfills her passion for helping organizations elevate engagement, retention, and collaboration. As Founder & President of Travers Training & Consulting, Rhonda leverages her thirty years of corporate expertise to share proven strategies, tools, and techniques equipping teams for excellence.

Rhonda is also committed to making a positive impact through community development. She has fulfilled multiple volunteer management and leadership roles for over twenty years.

When Rhonda is not walking 5k races with friends, she also enjoys spending time and watching sunsets at the Lake of the Ozarks with her husband, Paul.

After earning a Bachelor of Science in Accounting from Millikin University, Rhonda completed the Certified Internal Auditor (CIA), Certified Public Accountant (CPA), as well as Master Practitioner and Certified Trainer of Neuro-Linguistic Programming (NLP) certifications. Rhonda is also the #1 International Best-Selling contributing author of "Tenacity: The Deconstructing G.R.I.T. Collection".

Please scan the QR code to connect with this author.

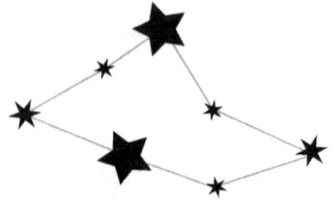

Maddie Smith

Windows to Growth

I have always loved sunlight. Whether indoors or outdoors, I made sure that whatever room I was in, I allowed the windows to capture the most sunlight possible. While others enjoyed waking up in a dark room, I prefer to be blasted with blinding rays. There is just something refreshing and new about sunbeams that sets the tone for your day. When thinking about sponsorship and mentorship, I began thinking of the windows I desperately uncover to see the beautiful world outside. A mentor and sponsor are like a window. A mentor allows you to see beyond your current circumstances and offers a broader perspective on opportunities and challenges. You have clarity and insight into possibilities. A sponsor is opening that window on a perfect day. The barrier is removed, and you are brought into a world you may not have been able to experience on your own. You smell the flowers, feel the wind, and are warmed by the sun that hits your face. You have never stepped outside, yet you experience the beauty that it offers. Through my journey, I have discovered that both a mentor and a sponsor can be a window to a guiding light to the opportunities and possibilities of your life and career.

Sponsorship

As someone who never thought they would be in the financial industry currently in one, I did not take a standardized test that said this would be the field for me. I found a company at an internship fair and gave them my resume. Through that action, I developed my first sponsor relationship. Of course, I did not know it at the time.

Bart is someone that I call my work dad. He was my host for my college internship and offered his office as a place for me to begin developing my skills and growing my career. Bart guided me on client attraction, analyst readings, and meeting procedures, for which I am grateful to this day. He also provided an ear as I cried about being called my first racist name in a professional space, he celebrated with me the first time I brought on a client, and he would tell me to get back to work when I was very easily distracted with conversation. I was not aware of everything he was doing while he was in his office, and his phone was on "Do Not Disturb." He was going to bat for me. He was being my sponsor.

As best as I can describe, the sponsor supports you in the rooms that you have not been able to enter. They mention your names in leadership meetings, headquarters networking events, and country club gatherings that my very small salary could not afford. When I failed an industry test, the first person I called was Bart. Through tears, I told him I had failed the test and felt like I had failed him. Of course, nobody wants to disappoint their dad—work dads included. While reassuring me, he told me, "I am not disappointed in you. We are going to try again." Within a few hours, I received a call from another department leader letting me know the steps to retake the test. By Monday, Bart was ready for me to begin studying again and checked in with me a minimum of once a week–but on average, every other day. He would ask my practice test scores and give me the contact information for people to call if I was stuck on a concept he could not answer. Bart updated leadership on my progress and how promising I was. He mentioned my name, ability, promise, and ambition, so I was not just another name but a living, breathing member of the meeting without physically setting my foot through the door.

I passed my tests, built my business, and eventually received a chance to open my own office. Through tearful goodbyes in a parking garage, I felt I was losing my comfort, a place I had called home for three years. Bart simply said, "We are still going to talk." Talk we did. He was able to meet my now husband before I did, as he was a church intern where Bart was a Deacon. We now sit together on the left and 4th pew from the front of the pulpit. He attended my wedding, and other than my parents and sister, he was the person I wanted to make sure I saw when walking down the aisle. He is a fixture in my life, not a moment, like I initially thought. He has encouraged my leadership, development, and acumen in the financial industry while pushing me to do more and improve. The wonderful thing about a sponsor is that you do not have to have a definite plan because, as Bart said, "We are going to get you there."

Mentorship

Like any millennial in the same position for five years; I got bored. I was coming to work and going through the motions. If someone were to ask me what I did at work that day, I would not have been able to answer. I decided to make a last-ditch effort before dusting off my resume and signing up for my company's mentorship program. I remember telling my office administrator then that I was going to pick someone completely different from me. He has over 25 years at the company to my five. He is a white man, and I am a black woman, and he was very established and successful compared to my, at the time, floundering mentality. His name is Ron, and when picking someone that I thought was so different from me, I chose someone that was just what I needed.

The first time I spoke with Ron was a learning and understanding meeting. He was in town attending an event at our headquarters and wanted to meet with me in person, considering he lives over 1,000 miles away. He asked me about my business goals, what I believed my pain points were in my business, and what activities I was currently doing.

When telling him how I was ready to jump ship, he simply said, "So, no pressure then?" He earned 10 points for the sarcasm. Ron then began to ask me what I love about my job, and I started naming my love for speaking in front of audiences and how I am very good at social media. Then, he asked me a simple question, "How often are you doing those things?" That simple question began my path to rejuvenating my passion and my mentorship relationship with Ron.

While a mentor can simply be described as someone who trains and advises, often someone who has been in the industry for a longer time, there is a part that is integral but overlooked. That is trust. From that simple question, my trust in Ron began to grow. As our monthly conversations continued, our weekly check-ins began to start. I remember running to my computer to tell him that I just received my first million-dollar check. I sent him a picture of my Golden Retriever Link, and he sent me an image of his Goldendoodle Ellie. I began to feel comfortable chatting with his office administrators, Kylie and Crystal, and updating them on my progress before they transferred me over to Ron. A trust has been built that allowed me to see him as my coach, advisor, counselor, and mentor.

As I write this in my office with two walls of windows, I reflect on the growth, lessons, and experiences in my career. My relationships with my mentor and sponsor have helped build the foundation of my career development. While windows can get dirty occasionally, I know that through these important relationships, I have developed the tools to maintain the clarity of the glass. Ron and Bart have been and will always be my windows.

Maddie Smith is a Saint Louis native and has built a career within the financial services industry. With a bachelor's degree in sociology and certification in paralegal studies, she brings her unique perspective to help educate individuals within her community professionally and socially. She is an Executive Board Member for Southside Early Childhood Center and an Advisory Board Member of the College of Humanities and Social Sciences for Webster University. She is a contributing author in Owning Your G.R.I.T: Women's Stories of Harnessing the Power of Growth, Resilience, Intention, and Tenacity. Her motto is, "The race isn't given to the swift nor the strong, but those who endure to the end."

Please scan the QR code to connect with this author.

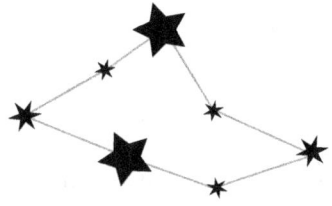

Krysta Grangeno

The Courage to Rise

Have you ever watched others quickly soar to new heights, while inside, you felt stuck in a continuous cycle of broken promises and self-sabotage? Have you ever chased after the trappings of success, only to have the dark shadows of generational trauma and statistical failure chase after you? For years, the fear of becoming just another statistic motivated me to hunt down and pursue every opportunity that promised to bring me closer to the ideal version of success. Mentors taught me the most promising strategies, and I quickly implemented them to help others and achieve our dreams. Through it all, I learned three key ingredients to attaining your dreams outlined in this chapter.

Generational Trauma

Generational trauma happens when psychological and emotional wounds are passed down from generation to generation. If this trauma is experienced early and often in life, the stress becomes toxic and disrupts the healthy development of a child's brain. Without mitigation, they develop maladaptive coping skills and adverse thought patterns, leading to people who survive in this world without ever truly thriving. There is often a longing for a different life but no understanding of what it looks like or even how to find the map to get there—a feeling of constantly spending life on a hamster wheel. You are constantly moving… but never truly advancing. A belief that certain dreams and positions are not even **FOR** you. Why dream big when life always lets you down?

This dance of desire and doubt swirls around our minds, driving us to chase every opportunity while simultaneously expecting the world to crumble around us, leaving us desolate once more. However, there is an opportunity to change the music.

There is always a moment in our lives when we must decide. We can continue on the familiar and less risky path **or** follow the intriguing yet terrifying one. Trauma amplifies our fight, flight, or freeze response, making change and risk challenging, so the familiar path often becomes the best option. You already know how to dance with the devils on the familiar path, so why risk the unknown?

There is nothing wrong with choosing the *familiar*. However, the *familiar* will not help you achieve your wildest dreams. You must take a leap of faith and navigate the uncharted waters to ultimately change your stars.

Embracing Your Power to Lead

For some who have been impacted by trauma, the notion of leading is equally scary and exhilarating. With leadership comes power, the ability to control your life instead of constantly being controlled, and the ability to create change. Inside, though, a moral battle rages because power was always used to cause physical, emotional, and/or psychological harm. Power is viewed as inherently evil.

However, what if I told you that power is simply the ***ability to act***? Throughout my career, I have been fortunate enough to learn from giants in the community organizing world, a world focused on ensuring those most impacted unite to create change. Mentors and personal conversations with individuals like Laura Barrett, Juan Soto, and Michael Kruglik (President Obama's mentor) taught me that leadership is more than a title or position. Leadership is our shared responsibility. Leadership is collectively using our power, individual talents, and connections to create a better world. In this, we all are leaders.

For two years, I partnered with church leaders, community members, and immigrant youth to build bridges between diverse communities and advocate for a more equitable world. We traveled across the country, from the state legislature to the halls of Congress, telling our stories and advocating for reform. We sat across the table from United States senators and representatives, debating issues and always leaving either deflated or inspired.

In one such meeting, I recall thinking, "What does this person have that we do not have? Why are they the ones making our country's laws when they appear to know little more than we do?" After days of pondering these questions, it finally hit me. In the course of a second, they decided to run for office. Power, therefore, is not inherently good or evil; it is simply the ability to choose to act. I then realized we could achieve our wildest dreams when we fully embrace our power.

Lifting Up Others

Unfortunately, advocating for systems change takes decades. Ready for a change, I began working in the field of family engagement, partnering with low-income families in Head Start/Early Head Start programs. A parent confronted me a couple of years into my position as the Family Partnership Director. She was furious that our programming kept parents returning for handouts instead of providing the tangible knowledge and skills needed to achieve their long-term goals. She challenged us to host successful people who could share their strategies and tools with parents instead of pushing conventional training with little reward. She desired access to opportunities, the unspoken tips and tricks that helped people achieve their dreams. Programming that she could use to lift herself from her current trajectory and onto a new life path.

It is unjust to those we serve when we sit in our offices and create programs amongst ourselves. True transformation happens when we create them alongside those who stand to benefit the most. As the years went by, she and other parents became my mentors. They were crucial to developing impactful programming. Together, we intertwined brain science and trauma-informed practice with concepts of power and leadership to create a school environment that strove to transform lives. We educated families on the impact of toxic stress on their children and ways to encourage healthy brain development. We co-created programs designed to address the two most significant stressors preventing families from positively interacting with their children: parenting, and finances. We organized family events at the school to build community. We even created leadership opportunities for families to get their input on the organization's policies, procedures, and programs.

Our parents became board members, funding advisors, entrepreneurs, homeowners, and parent representatives at the state level. With each level of success, local elementary schools approached me to discuss how to enhance their family engagement programs. This all developed because we had the simple goal of providing a welcoming, inclusive space for families to tap into their power and change their lives.

As time went on, though, a pattern began to emerge. In our highly supportive environment, some parents still hesitated to take advantage of the opportunities and gained little in return. This was when I realized that power and creating an environment full of opportunities were not enough. To truly become leaders in their own lives, they had to tap into their self-efficacy. Simply put, they had to **believe in themselves enough to achieve their goals.** This is where most people falter, and this is where I have often faltered.

Leaving a Legacy

I ran this transformational program for nine years before a family emergency turned my world upside down. Over the next three years, I took on more advanced roles, each one stretching my comfort zone and destroying the coping mechanisms I created early on to survive. It quickly became evident that to lead, I had to finally heal.

This is when the phrase from another powerhouse, Charlene Mack, crystallized for me. She says, "**The first revolution is internal.**"

This means that we must work on ourselves before we work on changing the environment around us. Suppose we carry our unhealed trauma, biases, prejudices, and cognitive distortions into our work and relationships. In that case, we risk infusing those maladaptive ideas into the very system we are trying to transform. Whether that system is an organizational culture, a program, a team, or even a law, we will inherently perpetuate inequities and continue to pass down generational trauma.

Therefore, we must heal. Healing not only allows us to be self-aware of our thoughts, feelings, and behaviors, it allows us to transform how we view the world. It brings light where there has only ever been darkness, and security where there has only ever been peril. We can take advantage of opportunities with intention and overcome the fear and anxiety of the unknown that consistently hold us back. We can finally embrace self-care and rest because we finally love ourselves, not because we are told it matters. We can finally break free from the curse of generational trauma and live the life of our dreams.

I once believed the legacy I wanted to leave to the world was one of creating space where ordinary people could do extraordinary things. I know now that my legacy is more grand. My legacy is creating space to break the cycle, changing our lives and those for generations to come.

Krysta Grangeno is a trailblazer driven by a passion for authenticity, empowerment, and values. With a Bachelor's in Social Work in hand, Krysta wasted no time diving into a community organizing internship through the Center for Community Change. Following graduation, she wholeheartedly embraced her role in the local affiliate of the Gamaliel Network, collaborating with church leaders to build bridges with immigrant communities, develop leaders, and influence national-level policies. Recognizing that long-lasting change requires a profound understanding of one's self and organizational systems, Krysta pursued and achieved her Master's in Nonprofit Management and ICF Certification as a Life, Leadership, and Executive Coach.

In her roles as an Operations Director, Chief of Staff, Sr. Manager of Statewide Initiatives, and Leadership coach, Krysta proves she is dedicated to making a difference in the lives of others. Her expertise extends to facilitating focus groups and leadership programs, operations, DEI, and program development. Through these endeavors, she tirelessly advocates for systemic change, addressing inequities, and creating opportunities for people to shine.

Please scan the QR code to connect with this author.

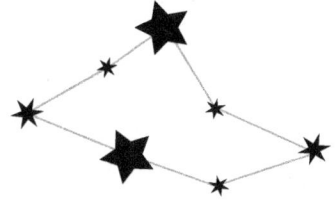

Mitch Meyers

Look Twice...Then Leap

Lead

Sometimes, the biggest risks lead to the most extraordinary rewards. When I left Corporate America, I started a marketing agency with two other guys. We built it from a small to medium-sized agency in four years. We were at a turning point in terms of size (whether to stay small or grow). I realized that to grow faster than we were would require resigning our largest client to take on one of their competitors. We were walking away from $3MM in annual billings to a new client without any guarantees of revenue. We made the decision to do it and embarked on a year of needing to hire an additional 120 employees to accomplish the work for the client while relocating to a larger space and executing 10x the volume of work we had previously handled. The new client ended up being more than $30MM annually which confirmed our need to change clients for growth. Looking back on this risky move, I now realize how that could have failed spectacularly. We were so lucky to have hired dedicated young people who shared our vision of effective work for our clients. We all worked incredibly hard to grow the company, maintain our desirous culture, and create award-winning work for our clients.

Lift

I once hired a diversity candidate to work at a small start-up I was leading. This woman practically stalked me for the job, as she was unhappy in her corporate work for a chemical company. She was very much into health and wellness and felt like she had sold her soul to her company. Truthfully, we didn't need a full-time employee at the time, but I brought her on due to her passion for our product and mission. After several years it was obvious the start-up could not support her role, and she confided in me that she really had the desire to open a small restaurant that served only organic, healthy food. Not only did I encourage her to take that step, but I personally invested in her endeavor. While it did not survive the pandemic, I was happy to see her follow her dream and try. I've lost money in worse investments. I felt this was an investment in a "human" whom I really cared about and her passion.

Leave a Legacy

In 2003 we sold our agency to the Interpublic Group, a global advertising and marketing company. I was very excited to retire and attempt that "Mother of the Year" award. For a few years, I spent time helping my kids as they were in high school. I also spent time building a second home in Colorado for family vacations. After a few years, my son was heading to college in Boulder, Colorado. When we were in the state visiting him, I realized an entirely new industry was starting in the state: legal medical cannabis. While I was not previously a cannabis user, I could not help but be fascinated by an entirely new industry springing up. I began researching the plant and its medicinal uses and was impressed with what natural plant medicine had to offer. Also, in researching the history of how the plant became illegal in the US, it was obvious it had nothing to do with its medical potential and everything to do with money and politics!

I knocked on many doors in the state to ask a million questions and see how the industry operated and who was benefiting. I could see people using this product to replace many types of pharmaceuticals, especially opioids. I also noticed something else that impacted me greatly. The people involved in the industry were a "community" with the desire to help people with natural plant medicine. They were happy to share their knowledge and expertise to help others get involved. This was completely different than the Corporate America I had worked in.

Back in my home state of Illinois, a legislative bill was making its way through the House and Senate to create a medical program for Illinois. I happened to meet a few individuals who had a desire to invest in a medical license in Illinois. I agreed to join forces with them to help with the legislation, as well as figure out how to apply for licenses. This was a great learning experience for me.

I had never been involved in lobbying and politics or anything having to do with healthcare. I invested thousands of hours researching every-thing about this new industry, and in 2014 won one of the dispensary licenses in Chicago. After getting it operational, I began to learn from our many patients how the plant helps them.

In 2015, the Department of Agriculture in Missouri made available two licenses for someone to cultivate, manufacture, and treat epilepsy patients. While it was anticipated this would not be a large, profitable business opportunity, I thought it would get me closer to the entire process of cultivating the plant and turning it into medicinal oil.

I did receive one of the two licenses and began the process of finding a grower and a scientist and building out a facility. This was an amazing experience getting to understand the disease of epilepsy and how the cannabis plant helps to stem seizures. Getting to meet these families with small children having 50-100 seizures per day was incredibly humbling.

When our CBD oil helped to stem or completely stop those seizures, it meant everything to our small staff. All the while we continued to learn about the benefit of the plants.

I spent a great deal of time educating neurologists around the state who now were being asked to allow their patients to get access to cannabis for their seizures. I learned more than I wanted to know about the pharmaceutical industry and clinical trials in this journey.

For several years, there had been a contingent of people who were attempting to organize and get a ballot initiative put together to bring full medical cannabis to the state of Missouri. Realizing that we had the first "legal" cannabis grown in the state in over 80 years, I took the opportunity to share my knowledge and the power of the plant with as many people as I could find. That included law enforcement, medical professionals, bankers, health insurers, media, and more. I spent 2 years guiding everyone through our facility treating it like a "display home". It worked to destigmatize the plant and to bring a focus on the medical modalities of cannabis.

At the same time, we formed a trade association to bring together everyone having an interest in participating in a state-wide medical cannabis program. This was fortuitous and has greatly impacted the success of the Missouri program. It brought all constituents together in the State that wanted to participate, prior to having anything to monetize. In that regard, everyone who ended up applying and getting licenses in the state had already become friends and were working together to bring the ballot initiative forward. Thus, when licenses were awarded, we were a group of Missourians who had been working together for 2 years, and that comradery still permeates our industry in the state. It is very different than other states and the rest of the country sees the benefit of it.

I then busied myself putting together a group of investors to apply for licensing. We applied for the maximum number allowed for one ownership group, thinking we would not win them all, but really wanted to win vertical licensing (cultivation, manufacturing, and retail.) We won all 10 licenses we applied for, which was good news and bad news! All 10 of these businesses had to be operational in 12 months or you could potentially lose the license.

While I was extremely busy fundraising, managing complicated construction projects, and hiring staff to manage a highly regulated, complicated industry, I was also setting an example to other women in the state and around the country as to the role a woman can play in this industry. As I had observed in Colorado, this was a brand-new industry springing up and, I felt, one that was uniquely suited to women.

I worked with several other women who wanted to get into the space and created We Are Jaine, a trade association to bring women into cannabis and provide training, mentorship, and jobs in a growing industry. I'm happy to say that we have created over 20,000 jobs in the state of Missouri, many of whom are fabulous women.

While I did not mean to get into another company on such a growth trajectory, it has been one of the most meaningful experiences in my career. What I have learned about myself over the last 68 years is that I am a life-long learner, and I sometimes can't get out of my own way. This last endeavor has given great hope and inspiration to many people and that is extremely rewarding!

After graduating with a Master's in Finance, and spending several years in the accounting and auditing field, Mitch realized that marketing and product development was her true calling. She was hired to introduce Bud Light for Anheuser-Busch. AB subsequently put her in charge of leading their new products group for 6 years. She was named AdWeek's Advertising Woman of the Year in 1996.

After leaving there, she and her partners formed a marketing and brand development agency, The Zipatoni Company, that worked with many Fortune 100 companies delivering strategic insights and business development programs. She and her partners built the agency to 350 employees, with offices in 5 states and $42 MM in revenue annually. They were acquired by IPG, the Interpublic Group in 2003.

Since that time, she has entered the medical cannabis industry receiving licenses in several states. Mitch's seasoned marketing expertise, coupled with her passion for the plant, products, and the patients, makes her one of the leading faces of the cannabis industry

.

Simone M. Cummings, PhD

The "Dirty" Word: Networking

Most of my friends like to joke that I'm connected to everyone—and yes, I do know a lot of people. However, knowing a lot of people doesn't mean I feel comfortable calling them all up and saying, "Hey, can you do me a favor?"

Too often, we think of networking as a transaction: you show up, introduce yourself, and then, just like magic—someone's reviewing your résumé and helping you land a job. As many of us have discovered, that approach doesn't work in the real world. Networking isn't about quick wins; it's about building genuine, long-term relationships. People are more likely to help you when they know and respect you.

In fact, networking is really just the process of building friend-ships, with the only difference being that networking tends to happen in work-related environments. And in the same way you wouldn't expect a new friend to help you move your entire apartment after one coffee date, you shouldn't expect someone from your professional network to provide you with a favor when they barely know you. Instead, nurture your connections with authentic engagement, and you'll find that your network, much like your friendships, will grow in meaningful ways.

Why Networking Gets a Bad Rap

Networking is often labeled a "dirty" word by individuals who attend events only to end up feeling awkward, insecure, and unhappy at the end of the evening because they have been unable to achieve their "networking" goals. True networking, however, is about making meaningful connections. It's not about collecting mountains of business cards (I just pitched about 200 of them) or LinkedIn contacts; it's about developing relationships based on mutual trust, respect, and friendship. When done right, networking can result in a circle of friends who can provide both professional and personal support.

How Do You Get Started?

We've all been there—walking into a room full of strangers, seeing people already engaged in conversation, and feeling like an outsider looking in. It can be very awkward and intimidating. The good news is that with a few tips and a shift in mindset, networking can become much easier and, dare I say—enjoyable. Below are some recommendations to help you build a strong, lasting network.

1. Arrive Early to Events

When attending an event where networking is likely to happen, arrive early. Showing up before the crowd gives you a chance to meet others before they've grouped into cliques with their friends. Early arrivals also tend to be more open to casual conversations. If you're particularly nervous about engaging in conversations with people you don't know, consider bringing a friend or colleague with you who is also looking to make connections.

2. Smile and Exude Warmth

It might sound simple, but a genuine smile and open body language can make a big difference in your interactions with others. People are naturally drawn to those who seem approachable and friendly. And smiling isn't just for appearances – it'll help you feel more confident and project that confidence to others.

3. Don't Be Afraid to Talk to People Who Are Different from You

It's easy to gravitate toward people who are similar to us—same age, background, or interests. However, some of your most valuable connections are likely to come from people who are different. My students often tell me they feel uncomfortable approaching older, more accomplished professionals because they don't think they'll have anything in common. However, many accomplished individuals love sharing their wisdom with those just starting out. Don't let differences in age, gender, or background intimidate you. You never know what you might learn from someone with a different perspective or what you can teach that person in return.

4. Take a Risk—Invite Someone to Coffee or Lunch

If you've had a meaningful conversation with someone and want to learn more about them, don't be afraid to extend an invitation. Suggest grabbing coffee or lunch to continue the discussion. People appreciate sincerity, and a one-on-one setting can lead to a deeper connection. Over the years, many people have approached me after I've given a talk or lecture to invite me for coffee, and I can honestly say I've never turned anyone down. Like me, most people are flattered by the invitation and happy to help if they see genuine interest.

5. Be Yourself

One of the biggest mistakes people make when networking is trying to be someone they're not. You don't need to put on a professional mask or impress people with your accomplishments. Just be you. People appreciate authenticity, honesty, and vulnerability. Remember, networking isn't about getting a job—it's about building a connection. When you let your personality shine, you're more likely to attract the right people into your network.

6. Shake Off Disappointments

Not every interaction will be a success, and that's okay. In any room, there will be people who are more interested in catching up with friends or colleagues and who may seem uninterested in meeting new people. Don't take it personally. Some may come across as cliquish or dismissive without even realizing it. The key is to keep moving forward. One awkward or unpleasant encounter doesn't define your networking journey!

7. Follow Up

If you had a good conversation with someone, send a follow-up message within a day or two, either through email or LinkedIn. Reference something specific from your conversation if possible. Consider using a personal customer relationship management (CRM) tool to track your contacts and interactions. CRMs can help you remember key details about your connections and ensure that you stay in touch over time. These apps ensure you never miss a key event related to a connection so that you can congratulate someone on a recent promotion, for example, or share an article related to a topic of mutual interest.

8. Build Your Network Before You Need It

One of the most important aspects of networking is timing. Don't wait until you need a job or favor to start building your network. By that point, it's too late. Think of your network as you would think of a plant. You need to tend to it on a somewhat regular basis, or it'll wither. If you nurture it, you'll see growth. When you invest time in building relationships early, you'll have a robust network to lean on when needed.

Final Thoughts: Redefining Networking

Networking doesn't have to be a "dirty" word. When you have a genuine interest in people and are open to forming new connections, networking becomes less about wanting to know individuals because of their potential to help you professionally and more about fostering meaningful relationships. And as you nurture your network over time, you'll find that opportunities will naturally come your way simply because of the relationships you've nurtured. So, the next time you hear the word "networking," don't cringe. Instead, think of it simply as an opportunity to make new friends.

Simone M. Cummings, PhD is the George Herbert Walker School of Business & Technology dean at Webster University. In this capacity, she provides leadership, management, and oversight for all aspects of the Walker School, including program planning and development; enrollment and retention; curriculum; hiring, training, and supervising faculty; accreditation; and community engagement—at the primary location in Webster Groves, Missouri, and across approximately eleven metro and international sites.

Simone M. Cummings, PhD earned a BSBA with a concentration in Marketing from Washington University, an MHA with a concentration in Finance from the Washington University School of Medicine, and a PhD in Health Policy and Administration from UNC-Chapel Hill. She actively serves on the boards of the Missouri Foundation for Health, St. Louis Children's Hospital, and the Missouri History Museum Subdistrict Commission. In her leisure time, she enjoys playing tennis and jazz piano. She is married with two daughters and a grand-dog.

Please scan the QR code to connect with this author.

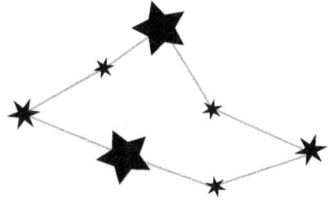

Jaime Nunnelee

Leave A Legacy:
Sales for Entrepreneurs

I believe in the power of mentorship in all areas of life—business, family, and peer relationships. Through this chapter, my goal is to empower others to succeed and thrive in their entrepreneurial journey. My legacy is rooted in practical, "how-to" guidance, reflecting the same qualities I value in my mentors.

Mentorship, to me, is about sharing knowledge and helping others along their journey. I've been fortunate to have several amazing mentors who've been critical to my success. I wanted to pay it forward by sharing insights on what I know best: business-to-business (B2B) sales. My hope is that you find key takeaways that bring you success and make sales more enjoyable.

I own a Direct Hire search firm and have over twenty years of sales and recruiting experience. When I graduated college, my main goal was to not move back in with my parents. The jobs I interviewed for offered a base salary below what I needed to pay the bills. I quickly realized that sales were the fastest way to support my independence. My first sales job was in print advertising, then software sales, before I was recruited into the staffing industry. Every year I met or exceeded my quota, and my paycheck was directly tied to my effort. One of my first mentors told me the fastest way to a raise is to go out and close more deals, so I did. That was it. I was hooked and never looked back.

My path to entrepreneurship started with a sales training program that had us write five-year personal, not professional, goals. I'd never really considered my long-term personal goals. That exercise was eye-opening and led me to the realization that the only way to achieve those goals was to start my own business. I founded NSR Talent in 2015 and have achieved every personal and professional goal I've set. The journey was full of highs and lows. Persistence, processes, and peers helped me stay the course and grow.

I'd tell anyone who's thinking about starting their own business to first learn and master your industry and build your network while working for someone else. It's paid training and invaluable. The lessons I learned and connections I made while working at other companies were key reasons why I was able to successfully transition to my own practice.

Once you start a business, you need revenue. Most entrepreneurs focus on sales last or dread getting started. The good news is that sales is a skill that can be taught. The secret is having a process and executing it. I've included a high-level sales process that can be customized for both product and service-based sales. This model is for B2B sales and is built on relationships and a traditional sales approach. If you're starting a business-to-consumer (B2C) business or e-commerce platform this can help but you'll want to include a digital marketing strategy.

Sample Sales Process
Step 1—Identify your Ideal Client Profile (ICP)/Target Clients
- Industry
- Geography
- Company Revenue (Fortune 500, mid-market, SMB)

- Number of employees

- Decision maker title (C-suite, Manager, Procurement, etc.)

Step 2—Plan

- Create a target list of 20 companies that match your ICP (spreadsheet for visibility)

- Identify 1-3 contacts at each company who buy your product/ service. Create an org chart per company if you sell to multiple departments.

- Create A, B, & C categories on your target list

  - o A—top 20 active company targets

  - o B—10 companies that move up to A next

  - o C—anyone that said "No", revisit when they have a change in leadership

Step 3—Prospect

- Create 9 unique scripts that are between 3-4 sentences max. AI can help create an outline and then customize it to your tone. Aim for polite persistence.

- Set your goals: how many attempts = a meeting

- Contact via LinkedIn, email, phone, referral, and networking every 3-5 days

- Schedule the next step in your database (up to 9 attempts per contact)

Step 4—Meet clients

- Know your metrics—how many client meetings lead to a contract/ close?

Step 5—Close

- Have a strong proposal/contract process, negotiation, and closing strategy

- Know how many deals you must close per month to hit your annual goals

Step 6—Retention

- Keep in touch with clients monthly, quarterly, or annually

Now that your process and target list are established, you're ready to execute. Along the way, things can—and likely will—go wrong, which is completely normal. Hang in there and trust the process. I've heard "no" far more often than "yes," but the wins are worth it. Below are lessons I've learned through failures, successes, and continual learning. I hope a few resonate with you and help you succeed as well.

General Sales Tips

Process—this is critical and bears repeating. Create or follow an established sales process for your industry, then execute. Make the calls, write the emails, and follow up.

Set Goals—both financially and activity-based. The industry term is KPIs (key performance indicators). You should have clear weekly, monthly, and annual goals written down. Hold yourself accountable or get an accountability partner.

Use your database—this is where most people fail. If you hate paper-work, do it anyway. Schedule prospecting calls, take call notes, create follow-up activities, and DO the follow-up calls.

Be consistent—an astounding number of sales professionals reach out once or twice to a potential client and never follow up. It can take between 6-9 attempts before a prospect gets back to you. Persistence and consistency win every time.

Don't be afraid to hear No—whoever you are calling is already not doing business with you. The worst thing that will happen is that they continue to not be a client. How amazing would it be if they said yes? Don't let fear of rejection stop you from getting started.

Get started—"Fake it 'til you make it" is really about confidence. Put on your confident face and know that you're an expert. They are meeting with you because they need whatever it is that you're selling. The conversation flows naturally when you're passionate about your company.

Mirror—follow your client's demeanor and approach, then listen. It's all about them, not you. Showing up and giving them your "pitch" without learning anything about them is an automatic failure. Ask questions, learn about how your companies align, and see if there's an opportunity to work together.

Communication—ask how your client likes to stay in touch. We have four generations in the workforce and some love calling while others prefer email or text. Note their preference in your database. Knowing what they prefer helps achieve the fastest response.

Don't discount—as the business owner, I was frequently asked for discounts. It took my mentor reminding me that my rates are industry standard and that my competition won't discount, so why did I? Know your worth and stand firm on your rates.

Retention—add a personal information section to your database and add details about their hobbies, favorite sport, drink, family, dog, etc. Check in quarterly or annually depending on your industry (schedule the call in your database) and get to know more about them personally and their business needs.

Focus—identify the areas that you can control (your target clients, activity, messaging, etc.) and let go of everything outside of your control. Sales is a roller coaster but if you stay on the track and focus on your goals, the results will come.

Strategic Partnerships—invest time and build real relationships with strategic partners. They are other sales reps or business owners who work with your target clients but don't compete with you. I recommend having 2-4 that you meet with quarterly. Examples in my industry are other staffing firms that focus on IT, finance, legal, marketing, etc., sales training companies, resume writers, etc. Building key relationships with these people is the best source of referrals and are amazing resources to help and mutually grow.

Network—I'm an introvert and still attend 2-4 networking events a month. In-person networking is fundamental in service-based and commoditized industries. Research groups that are specific to your industry commit to 1-2 events per month initially.

Community—have a mentor and entrepreneur peers who you can go to for guidance and advice. Having a trusted community of these people has saved me money, time, and my sanity year after year. I'm in three groups that meet monthly, and I find value in each. One is all recruiters (peers), one is sales reps in other industries (strategic partners), and one is business owners (mentors).

Opportunity—always say yes to a 20-minute call or meeting. Sometimes it's those unexpected meetings or connections that come back to you tenfold. I'll always take a client or candidate referral even if they are outside of my niche. I typically refer them to one of my strategic partners, which helps everyone. Being open-minded and collaborative goes a long way.

Adapt—be ready to pivot when needed. Whether it's a pandemic or economic dip in your industry, successful people are resourceful and know how to pivot with the market. Identify the industries that are benefiting from the shift and target those accordingly.

Opt-out—it's ok to walk away from clients or partners who don't align with your core values. If they are rude or difficult, never take it personally. It's rarely about you. I know business owners and sales reps who increase their prices for problematic clients. It's genius. That allows the client the opportunity to decline moving forward, or you're paid extra for dealing with them.

Be a continual learner—if you're still with me, you're ahead of your peers. Listen to sales podcasts, follow industry leaders, read books on specific topics, etc....Things change rapidly, and successful people are always learning ways to make themselves better.

Be human—people work with people they like. Be professional, but authentic. It goes a long way.

I also surround myself with people who are high achievers and highly recommend it. If everyone you know is complaining about the economy or offering up excuses, find a new circle. Entrepreneurs and top sales reps pivot when outside factors impact their end goal. Being resourceful, adaptable, and open-minded is key. In the end, success comes from preparation and execution.

If you're interested in diving deeper, or for recommendations on tools, my contact information is on the Linktree for this book. I welcome the opportunity to meet you!

Jaime Nunnelee is the President of NSR Talent, an Executive Search Firm specializing in building high-performing teams in sales and human resources. A Missouri State University graduate with a Bachelor's in Marketing, she has over 20 years of experience in sales and recruiting.

A St. Louis native, Jaime is actively involved in the community and is a member of several local human resources, sales, and nonprofit organizations. She partners with local universities to mentor students on resume preparation and mock interviews. Jaime is passionate about connecting businesses with top talent and fostering relationships that drive success.

She is married with two children and a dog. In her free time, Jaime enjoys traveling, Pilates, hiking, reading, and spending quality time with friends and family.

Please scan the QR code to connect with this author.

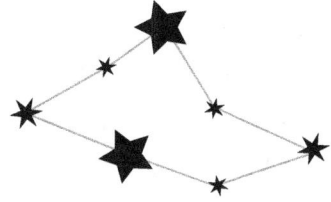

Dr. Nadine Alameh

Resilience—Ambition—Empathy—Leadership

Life truly works in mysterious ways. I never imagined I would be where I am today, leading global organizations in the hot, pervasive field of geospatial. I was once asked about the turning point in my life that got me here. I realized that there were many turning points:

- **Saying YES to an MIT scholarship.** This meant leaving my family: a single mom who raised me, my brother, and my sister on her own during the tough 20+ years of civil war in Lebanon.

- **Moving to Washington DC** to help my deaf brother get adjusted to life outside of Lebanon as he started his journey at Gallaudet University. This decision ended up landing me at NASA working on the coolest research with satellite data and geospatial tech.

- **Saying YES to start up** the US office of a British company, a decision that landed me in the Aviation domain—a new domain to me, yet within 3 years our hard work to modernize that industry paid off to earn us international innovation awards, not to mention becoming profitable.

- **Resigning from an amazing job** that was designed for me at Northrop Grumman to become the first female CEO of the Open Geospatial Consortium—the largest consortium of geospatial tech organizations—at just the right time to make geospatial/location

125

part of every system and domain on earth (and space!) which landed me the Women in Tech of the Year award.

- **Jumping on the opportunity to lead a brand-new research institute**—an opportunity poised to build a different type of research institute—one that combines geospatial, Artificial Intelligence, cloud computing, and data science to have an impact on climate, disasters, health, national security and more, all via partnerships with industry, government, and amazing researchers worldwide.

To me, the key is to be open to opportunities, to look for the challenges, and to not be afraid to make a move in every step of my journey. I reflect on 6 themes.

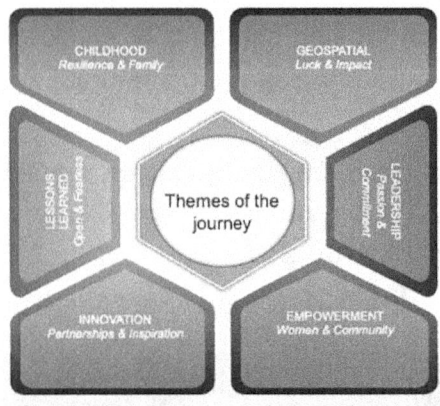

➢ CHILDHOOD. Story of resilience and power of family support

➢ GEOSAPTIAL. Role of luck and opportunity for impact.

➢ LEADERSHIP. Path of passion and commitment to success.

➢ EMPOWERMENT. Power of community building and growing our women network.

➢ INNOVATION. Strength of partnerships and inspiring pushing boundaries.

➢ LESSONS LEARNED. To being fearless, open, and authentic.

On Childhood—One thing is for sure; I don't wish my childhood on anyone. We grew up during the Lebanese Civil War. That means constant bombing, loved ones dying, moving from one shelter to the next, no electricity, no water, and minimal schooling for starters. My mom reminded me of how to reach family EVERY time she went out to buy groceries because it was always a risk that she'd never make it back home. I remember how my mom made us all sleep on the same mattress in the hallway. In case our apartment was hit, we'd at least all die together. We all envied my brother for being deaf because he could at least sleep during the heavy bombing nights. No kid should grow up in such circumstances. There are several silver linings: (1) the family, neighbor, and friends' bonds during times like this are unbreakable, (2) one's empathy towards others develops quickly—we MUST help each other as human beings! (3) resilience—after you experience such circumstances, EVERYTHING is easier. If it's not life or death, we can figure out how to address any business challenges. As a leader, that has been a very helpful perspective and ingredient for success.

On Geospatial—I love geospatial now, but 20 years ago I didn't even hear about it. When I selected Computer Engineering as my undergraduate major, I had never seen a computer. I had never even had a phone growing up. As luck would have it, MIT was awarding four scholarships to the top four students at the American University of Beirut (AUB) in various fields—Geographic information systems, construction management, finance, and multimedia. As one of the top four seniors, I got one of those scholarships. We didn't know who got which field. We didn't care. We had an all-paid path to MIT, the BEST engineering school in the world, and that was all we needed to say YES. I got the Geographic information systems "ticket", and it ended up changing my life. Turns out Geospatial is AMAZING. It's all the data that deals with the Earth—from satellites, from sensors, and from people about all aspects of our lives, from natural resources to built-environment, to all sorts of applications. I ended up specializing in using geospatial technology and sharing information to connect across all this data and all these domains.

On Leadership—I don't know how I ended up being one of the leaders in my field and the CEO/President/Founder of several organizations along the way. I feel like I end up leading because, when I believe in something, my passion is UNSTOPPABLE. I BELIEVE in the power of geospatial. Looking back, I see my leadership style centered around my passion for attracting similarly passionate and committed people. This leads to great things! Combining passion with an endless thirst to solve hard problems makes geospatial an even more attractive field because the problems that we are solving impact us as human beings on this planet. I'm really proud that my work has led me to be part of policy discussions: In the US as part of the National Geospatial Advisory Committee to advise on shaping the national geospatial data infrastructure for maximum leverage and impact, and in the United Nations as part of UN-GGIM to advise on bridging the geospatial capability gap between the developed and developing world. Having grown up in Beirut, Lebanon, I'm grateful for the opportunity to push this agenda forward at the highest levels of influence.

On Innovation—I am fascinated by new technology, and I get excited about "playing" with it. I'm a geek. I'm in the right field, as geospatial practically incorporates all sorts of techs. I've had the privilege of shaping and driving many of the geospatial innovations. I was one of the first ones to implement and advance web services for earth observation data. I'm particularly proud that my prototype was used in the 9/11 rescue efforts to get and overlay data from multiple sources over New York. This was one of the reasons I was able to get the US "green card" as a person of extraordinary ability. This thirst for innovation continued with me leading OGC during the transition from web services to mainstream APIs—so that YOU can integrate location data with any other type of data out there. Having two kids, I am very excited that I was one of the first in the industry to work on bridging the gaming and geospatial industries. My Metaverse podcast with Patrick Cozzi (Cesium) and Marc Petit (Epic Games) remains one of my favorites. I was excited to meet Neal Stephenson (who coined the term Metaverse) and participate with him in one of the first panels on the topics of geospatial and the metaverse. Now, it's Artificial Intelligence time. AI is the only way we can make sense of the Terabytes of data collected by the 3500+ satellites orbiting Earth. I'm excited that, as a geospatial community, we are supporting the concept of "talking to Earth"—think ChatGPT but for Earth. How cool!

On Empowerment—The reason I got excited about being part of this book is because it's a way to (1) connect with other amazing women all over the world, and (2) hopefully inspire some young professionals to pursue their passions despite the challenges of being women in technology. I have lived and unfortunately continue to live and observe the challenge of being taken seriously in meetings with all (usually older) men, the challenge of having to prove myself over and over in order to be heard, and the challenge of feeling like I fit in, because as women leaders in technology, we have very few role models we can connect with. My solution to these challenges has been to build my network of amazing women. My network of women in the geospatial field continues to not only inspire me but to effectively support me. I think the pathway to true full integration in the business place is via such strong networks of leaders and influencers. It doesn't stop at geospatial. When I first moved to the Washington DC area and was looking for new female friends, I had to look beyond the workplace where there were very few women to start with. I landed with Jazzercise, I became an instructor and franchisee in 2004 to meet and empower women on a totally different level, and I never looked back. Combining my passion for dancing and my passion for lifting other women up makes me happy every time I step on the Jazzercise stage to teach a class. Over the last 20 years, my students have become my best friends. We have become each other's cheerleaders and support network.

On Learning—I love how life works and how our stories continue with always learning and always growing—together! I'm usually asked about what I would say to young professionals and future women leaders.

My advice is: TRUST YOUR GUT! I look back at many tough periods in my life. In these moments, I didn't follow my gut. My second advice is to be fearless. I think that's been one of the ingredients of my adventure so far. What's the worst that can happen? If it's not life or death, it's something that can be figured out. Go for the opportunity, try something new, push yourself. It's worth it—EVEN if things don't work out. That's how we gain experience. Experiencing the good, bad and the ugly makes us who we really are.

My last bit of advice is to surround yourself with genuine people and to keep helping others. That's how we grow our network, how we grow a supportive community, and what goes around actually comes back around. That's the beauty of life. Let's lead, lift, and leave a legacy—together!

Dr. Nadine Alameh is often introduced as the cheerleader for the geospatial sector. If you've used a map, checked the weather, or marveled at NASA data, you've experienced a tech that Nadine has touched one way or another. She has established herself as a global leader for the advancement and impact of geospatial/location technology.

She focuses on fueling a revolution of geospatial innovation and AI in her current role as the Executive Director of the Taylor Geospatial Institute. Before TGI, Nadine was the CEO of the Open Geospatial Consortium. Her leadership positions have ranged from senior advisor to NASA, Chief Architect at Northrop Grumman, and the founder of startups.

Dr. Alameh has received multiple leadership awards: the 2024 St. Louis Business Journal Most Influential Businesswoman award, the 2023 Annual Women in Technology Leadership award, the 2022 Geospatial World Diversity Champion award, and the 2019 Geomatics Canada Leadership Award.

Nadine holds a Ph.D. and 2 M.S. degrees from MIT; and a B.S. in Computer Engineering from the American University of Beirut, Lebanon.

Please scan the QR code to connect with this author.

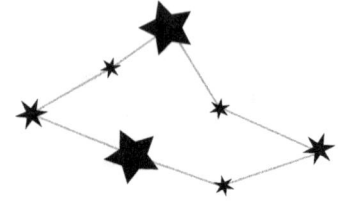

Betsy McBride

Culture is Key

To serve others so lives are transformed
— The Why Statement for The Gund Company

The Gund Company provided my employment, but I wondered how long it would last when I realized a very important order did not ship on time. Unfortunately, I lost my head and took out my frustration on a coworker. We had it out right there on the floor. At the time, TGC was working on a new way to do business that included a shift in culture. The resulting empathy I received from the leaders in the company was transformative.

If I had considered the vision statement before this event, I would have thought that it sounded like an odd statement coming from a company that makes insulators for electrical equipment. On this specific Friday morning, the only transforming I was thinking about was how fast I would be fired. Within the hour of my incident, the phone in my office rang. The name RICH GUND was displayed on the caller ID, in all caps, and I cringed in anticipation for the worst. With a heavy heart, I picked up the receiver and said hello. To my surprise, Rich simply said, "I hear you are having a hard time with Bob; how can I help?" Those are powerful words, "How can I help?" Asking questions like this is how TGC is transforming lives.

A few days before the "incident" as it has come to be known, I had put an enormous amount of pressure on myself to complete an order. My task was to get several R&D parts machined and shipped to the customer by a certain time. Resources were scarce and the shop was busy with current orders for good customers. The facility I worked at specializes in turning orders in a short amount of time for the generator repair industry. The company has the experience necessary to deliver six-sigma quality parts to our customers as they need them. Unfortunately for me, the resource needed to complete my parts was also needed to machine parts for a long-time customer, decisions were made, and I was on the losing end. I was devastated when I realized my customer wasn't supported and immediately started my after-action report which led to the incident.

I had only been in the position for a few months and was desperate to prove my worth. I took this job after attending the Executive MBA program at Washington University in St. Louis after being a stay-at-home mom for 15 years. Though I had jobs throughout my stay-at-home career and worked in other industries where people treated each other with respect, my attitude toward manufacturing still clung to its roots from my years at an automotive company right out of undergrad. The automotive industry in the late 90's and early 00's was rough to say the least. I had adopted the stance that he/she who screamed the loudest won along with the motto never admit you were at fault. It wasn't the healthiest environment to grow up in. -

Missing my deadline left me feeling like a complete failure. I felt like I couldn't contribute anything to the shop, couldn't do the job I was hired to do, couldn't communicate effectively, and couldn't even get along with my coworkers. I was contemplating my next career move, but doubting any company would want to hire me. Then I received the call that would change my perspective on many things. Rich's empathetic words changed my trajectory. "How can I help?" changed my mind about my perceived value at TGC.

TGC is a family-owned manufacturing company founded over seventy years ago by Ed Gund. He passed the torch to his son and then grandsons who grew the business many folds. When the third generation took control, they came to understand that there is a better way to run a business. They introduced a concept that would eventually transform my life. They created a plan to follow that they depicted with a "north star". This "north star" includes the three pillars and eight core values. The three pillars are Take Care of Each Other, Take Care of the Customer, Take Care of Business. The pillars work like legs on a three-legged stool each must be followed equally for the company to prosper. The eight core values; Connection, Teamwork, Integrity, Performance, Passion, Growth, Trust, and Respect were created to help guide employees to treat each other like family. It's a way to create a culture that mimics a small family business in a multinational company.

The pillar, Taking Care of Each Other (TCoEO), is at the top of the "north star". This is not by chance. While each pillar is equal and necessary, placing TCoEO at the top of the star emphasizes the importance of a culture that supports employees in the company. I appreciate this pillar most because I believe this is the catalyst for the reason Rich reached out to me.

To recognize and serve others so that lives are transformed...
Reconocer y servir a los demás para que las vidas sean transformadas...

Note: this is the North Star that TGC developed, and I have permission to use it in this chapter.

When he called me to encourage rather than chastise, Rich suggested that we meet for lunch the next day. He was able to give me perspective on what was expected of me in my position. We had set up a standing lunch meeting monthly for several of the following months where we discussed the pillars, the core values, and how they determined the culture of the company. He answered questions I didn't even know to ask.

Culture isn't just created out of thin air. Employees need guidance and a safe place to practice positive exchanges when trying to solve issues. TGC has tailored a program called Listen Like a Leader (LLaL) to meet their cultural standards. This program is designed to train employees in the skills needed for positive problem-solving interactions. The course outlined the culture the company was striving to create. The objective is to help employees understand how personality profiles provide insights into behavioral tendencies. It spells out how each different personality can bend their natural approach to communication to work with other communication styles in a positive way. It covers the communication cycle and the challenges of human communication. It teaches empathetic listening as well as accountability with compassion. The course demonstrates how the traditional thoughts on the leadership structure with the leader on top dictating to the masses is upside down. TGC culture supports servant leadership which makes room for the leader to be at the bottom of the triangle creating space to help their employees and coworkers grow. When adopted, the intent of the tenets of LLaL is to transform the culture in this highly competitive manufacturing environment into a supportive work environment.

In the immediate days following the incident, after Rich reached out to me, I became aware that I needed to adjust my attitude if I wanted to stay at this company. I truly took some time to search my soul. I asked myself if I would be able to work within the parameters of servant leadership. Was I willing to do the work necessary to transform from reactive to proactive problem-solving? Was there was a world where Bob and I could get along? Is the cultural picture they are painting the place where I want to work? If I commit to this culture, can I grow?

The answer was yes. Yes, I could adopt the actions required for servant leadership by listening more and talking less. I could redefine my mission as a manager by providing more resources to help my team grow. I could listen first and solve problems without casting blame by coming to the conversation with an open mind as opposed to a predetermined solution. Turns out I could even get along with Bob, who has become a friend. Bob too put in the time and effort to change his ways to align with the culture the company was promoting. Most companies have cultural rules to guide that organization. The difference I found at TGC is that the leadership made space to practice. We were given time to work through dialogs about difficult conversations with our coworkers. My colleagues were excellent teachers as we worked through the process. More impressive is that these lessons are implemented at every level of the organization. As time passed, indeed I was able to grow in my leadership abilities within the company.

My life was transformed the minute Rich Gund took the time to pick up the phone and say, "How can I help you?" This simple act from Rich exemplified the importance of culture in a company. He is living the message. A culture that facilitates positive interactions between coworkers makes the workplace better. I was the beneficiary of a company that values a positive culture. Rich's act of kindness at a time when I expected censure was transformative. The Gund Company has a true understanding of how a well-defined culture is key to its success.

Source: The Gund Company Culture Orientation presentation.

Betsy started her work career in the automotive industry after graduating from Indiana University. While working for one of the "Big Three," she earned her first master's degree. This was followed immediately by a fifteen-year hiatus to be a stay-at-home mom to three sons. She enjoyed all her years as a scout leader and volunteering at the school and church. During this time, she met her best friends through the "Play Group" and later the best "Book Club" ever. In preparation to return to the paid working world, she earned an EMBA through Washington University in St. Louis. Her favorite activity is to travel and enjoys experiencing new cultures in foreign lands. She loves her husband, Lincoln, and is looking forward to the adventures to come.

Please scan the QR code to connect with this author.

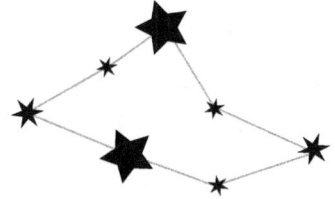

Dr. Peggy Petralia

The Journey to Motivation Starts with You

As a young medical student in 1987, I relished lively conversations with my classmates, many of whom were equally eager to finish our studies and make a difference in the world. Between classes, we often discussed and debated current events. One day, as we deliberated a proposal to mandate free AIDS treatment for all Missouri residents, I argued that it could pose a significant economic burden on the state. A classmate responded sharply, "Peggy, you can't just let these people die on the street. *You're fortunate because you were born motivated.* Not everyone is as lucky as you." That statement stopped me in my tracks. Born motivated? Was that even possible? "No," I replied firmly. "I wasn't born motivated—no one is born motivated. But I was fortunate to have two incredible parents who taught me the importance of earning my place in the world and contributing to society. So yes, in that sense, I am lucky."

We are all born into unique circumstances, and the playing field is undeniably uneven. This disparity raises an important question: where does motivation really come from? Why do some people overcome immense obstacles and succeed against all odds, while others, born into privilege and opportunity, accomplish little or even become society's outcasts? Motivation is the force behind our actions, pushing us toward our goals. It stems from both conscious and unconscious processes, influenced by internal factors like hunger and energy levels, as well as external forces such as rewards, punishments, and the people around us. This is why mentorship holds such transformative power. It has the ability to shape our path and redefine what we believe is possible.

Discerning your purpose

I believe there are essential, non-negotiable steps needed to derive true motivation and accomplish successful goal completion on our path to greatness. Yes, greatness. The first step is to uncover your purpose—a task that is neither simple nor swift. It's a journey you'll likely revisit for years as you navigate the other steps, and your answers may evolve over time. Consciously think about what motivates you and the choices you make. I remember being eight years old, spending hours staring out of my parents' kitchen window, trying to piece together how the world worked and why. I questioned everything, even the basics: why did our bodies need water to survive instead of something like Kool-Aid? Inevitably, my thoughts would turn inward, wondering about my true purpose and what God might be calling me to do with my life.

At eighteen, I understood why our bodies didn't run on Kool-Aid, but I was not much closer to understanding what my intended purpose was. It didn't matter. Being raised Roman Catholic, my parents had instilled in me a strong foundation of core values which remain my compass for the decisions I make today.

The Importance of Relationships

I was incredibly fortunate to be born into a family where I had two strong, loving parents who became my first and most influential mentors. Through their teachings and example, I learned to place God at the center of my decisions and to understand that one of our greatest purposes on this earth is to build meaningful relationships and learn how to love one another.

My journey took an unexpected turn when, at the age of four, I was diagnosed with juvenile rheumatoid arthritis. The disease affected my right knee and left ankle, leaving me unable to traverse across the street to my best friend's house. The treatment was intense: weekly injections and blood draws for 20 weeks, followed by monthly visits for years. On some visits to the doctor, I endured painful joint aspirations where a long needle would be inserted into my joints to remove fluid and inject steroids. Although the nurses and doctors were kind, I remained terrified at my appointments. Despite this, I was expected to behave perfectly. Any outburst, tears, or complaints would result in an immediate reprimand and punishment at home. Looking back, this experience taught me resilience. I share it with you to illustrate that while life's struggles may shape us, they don't have to define us. The choice is ours.

I valued making my parents proud, so I worked hard to overcome the pain and blend in with my peers at school. When asked to be the poster child for the Arthritis Foundation, much to my mother's disappointment, I refused. At the time, I just wanted to be seen as a "normal" kid, not someone defined by an illness. Where did my strength come from? It came from God, my loving family, and the remarkable teachers who mentored me throughout grade school and high school. Under their guidance, I began to uncover my talents and discovered how to rise above the perceived injustice of my health challenges. Their belief in me helped to instill a sense of hope and empowered me to see beyond my struggles. These early influencers whom I intentionally sought out, had a profound and lasting effect, shaping the person that I am today.

Making a Plan

The next step is to consciously reflect on what motivates you. Take time to examine the choices you make each day—both big and small, even those that seem insignificant. This self-reflection will help clarify your values and priorities, making larger decisions easier as your path becomes more evident.

As you identify both your talents and limitations, begin aligning them with your core values and create a plan. Ask yourself: What legacy do I want to leave behind? What steps must I take to walk that path? Start with small steps. Remember, Rome wasn't built overnight. In today's world, where technology is at our fingertips and Google provides instant answers, it's easy to grow impatient all too quickly. No one understands better the need for instant gratification than a former emergency room physician such as myself. For those of us who are Type A individuals and may struggle with this, it's crucial to practice the virtue of patience. Sometimes, I intentionally delay pouring that first cup of java in the morning, forcing myself to complete a task first as a practice in delayed gratification.

Remember, your plan is not set in stone. Timelines can—and should—be adjusted as circumstances evolve. A plan is simply a tool to keep you on track. Finding a mentor should be an essential part of your plan. Look for someone who is already achieving what you're striving for and reach out to them.

While it's important to remain open to changes, it's also vital to set up some guardrails to keep you from veering too far off course. For example, one of my challenges is that I struggle with saying no or disappointing others, which often leads me to overextend myself. This can be counterproductive to my success. To avoid my instinct to immediately try to assist, I've established a "second ask" guardrail. Here's how it works: I don't allow myself to respond until I've seen the request for a second time.

This practice has helped me limit my extracurricular commitments and focus on where my help is truly needed.

Above all, remember to stay centered. It's essential to keep refilling your own cup—mind, body, and soul—so you have something to give to others. Additionally, you will be less likely to burn out and more likely to keep motivated. Whenever my father noticed I was trying to take on too much, he would remind me, "Peg, take care of yourself first, because if Mama goes down, the whole family goes down." In his own way, he served as an unintentional but invaluable guardrail. Sometimes, we become so hyper-focused and tunnel-visioned that we lose perspective. Our loved ones may have a wider-angle lens and can help us step back, slow down, and realign.

The Importance of Trust

Another key to staying motivated lies in the trust you establish with others—and with yourself. What exactly is trust? Trust is the belief that someone or something is reliable, that they will act and follow through as they say. It's a fundamental building block to all relationships and an essential ingredient for success. Babies are born with a natural instinct to trust, in which they seek to form strong bonds with their caregivers. However, this innate trust will be shaped by life experiences. The consistency with which a child's needs are met, along with broken promises, manipulation, or repeated demonstrations of unreliability can all profoundly influence how easily someone places trust in others.

If someone repeatedly experiences breaches of trust—or worse, emotional and/or physical abuse by a caregiver/trusted loved one—it can deeply impact their ability to trust, not only the individual at fault but others as well. Recognizing and addressing these influences is a crucial step in fostering healthier, stronger relationships and for building confidence in our own ability to trust ourselves and in our instincts. Without the ability to trust yourself and others, it becomes much harder to distinguish truth from the myths or lies you might tell yourself. This makes you more vulnerable to accepting and being influenced by fallacies that can distort your reality. As a result, you may develop a misguided sense of priorities.

For me, the single most important way to stay grounded in truth is through prayer and meditation. My resolute belief in a God who loves me unconditionally gives me the confidence to trust that He will guide me toward the right decisions. Accepting that my plan may not be the same as His has carried me through some of life's most disappointing and heartbreaking moments. This perspective has taught me to pause and ask, "Is this the right path?" when I find myself in a relentless struggle to make something happen. It is the trust in myself and my judgment that I've cultivated through the years that allows me to at times, act with blind faith— to accept that I can trust in God's plan without fully understanding why things unfold as they do. This faith enables me to view failure not as an end, but as a part of the journey, giving me another opportunity to learn and grow.

Owning it

The final, and perhaps most important, element is accountability. When you truly take ownership of your plan, embracing both its successes and its failures, you're far more likely to stay motivated and committed to seeing it through. It's crucial not to confuse control with accountability. Control is about exerting authority to manage and regulate actions, whereas accountability is about taking ownership of your choices and accepting responsibility for their outcomes.

When a plan fails or goes off track, it's essential to have the insight to reassess, take responsibility, and make the necessary adjustments. There is no greater way to gain the respect and trust of others than by being humble enough to acknowledge and own your mistakes. If you find yourself stuck or not making progress, take time to reflect and identify what's holding you back. Develop a strategy to overcome the obstacle. Remember, roadblocks are not just challenges—they're opportunities for deeper understanding and personal growth. Embracing them with the right mindset can lead to even greater success.

No one is born motivated. Motivation must be cultivated, and it comes from within. *It is a journey that starts with you.* No one else can give you the motivation you need to achieve your goals and live your dream. Others may serve as inspiration, but the drive to act must come from your own desire and will to achieve greatness. Think about the world we live in—what do you want to accomplish? By investing time in discerning your purpose, creating a plan, and committing to it, you'll find yourself well on your way to greatness. Mentors can serve as powerful catalysts to elevate our journeys, and by being a mentor yourself, you are paying it forward and helping others reach their potential.

Dr. Peggy Petralia is an Osteopathic Family Physician who began her career as an emergency room physician in South Texas in 1992. She returned to St. Louis in 1995, where she continued practicing in the emergency room for over twenty years. In her current role as Senior Medical Director for a national health plan, she leads a team of Medical Directors and has been instrumental in developing a mentorship program for the medical affairs staff. Her personal values are deeply rooted in serving God, her family, and acting as a positive role model for others. As a dedicated wife and mother of four young men, she has enjoyed hosting several exchange students from Chile, traveling, boating, and spending quality time with her family. Guided by her philosophy and inspired by Philippians 4:8-9, she strives to live a life of integrity and purpose.

Please scan the QR code to connect with this author.

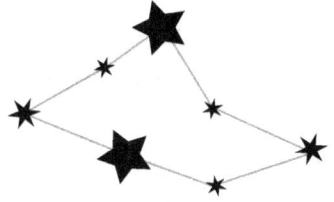

Lindsay Skredenske

All Roads Lead to Luke

Motherhood isn't always the picture-perfect journey I'd envisioned. It's messy, exhausting, and often overwhelming. Amidst the diaper changes and bedtime stories, a profound shift is occurring. My son, Luke, is my most demanding teacher, pushing me to grow in ways I never anticipated. He's the driving force behind my desire to leave a legacy. All roads in my life have led to Luke. He is a testament to the truth that not every wish should be granted. Everything works out as it should, but sometimes it's hard to understand in the moment.

My husband and I yearned to be parents. After several years of trying, we sought fertility treatment. IVF offered hope. Simultaneously, my husband's mother battled uterine cancer. A fighter, she eventually became cancer-free. That wish was granted. We celebrated with a family cruise to Alaska. There, my father-in-law suffered a heart attack. Thankfully, he survived but required a costly medevac to get home. Our family and friends rallied and raised the funds. That same week, our fertility clinic was bought out threatening to take our eggs to Chicago. A wish was seemingly snatched away with this devastating blow. With our doctor's help, we recovered them and continued treatment.

Then, while I was pregnant with Luke, my mom, the kindest woman I know and the mother I aspire to be, was diagnosed with breast cancer.

It was a terrifying time. Luckily, it was caught early. She underwent a double mastectomy and is now cancer-free. She even got her tubes out the morning Luke was born. The reason she found the cancer early was that she ran a ton of medical tests to ensure she'd be healthy for her grandson. Even in this difficult moment, all roads led to Luke.

Through it all, I knew it was time to prioritize family and define my own desires: to be a mom, a wife, and work somewhere I was proud of. I confided in a friend at Make-A-Wish, and a position was available. I was offered the job, even after disclosing my ongoing IVF treatments. They valued family. The week I started at Make-A-Wish, I took a pregnancy test. Posting negative results, this wish was deferred. In hindsight, I'm grateful. That wouldn't have been Luke.

The first implant failed. It was heartbreaking, but a few months later, another implant succeeded. Though not on my original timeline, this wish was granted. That baby is Luke. He's the best thing that's ever happened to my husband and I. Had we conceived earlier, Luke wouldn't exist. The setbacks, the detours—they all led me to him.

Before Luke, I valued efficiency and control. Motherhood shattered that illusion. It demands flexibility, adaptability, and surrender. It teaches me the profound connection between Luke's well-being and my own. His joy fuels mine.

This flexibility permeates my life, softening my edges and deepening my connections with others. At the Make-A-Wish organization, my empathy for the families we serve has intensified. Wishes are more than words; they're embodiments of fierce parental love and unyielding hope. It's less about granting a wish and more about understanding the "why."

Luke reinforces that not every wish is granted, nor should it be. Sometimes, the hardest decisions are the most loving. Even in saying no, we can offer hope and connection. Everything works out as it should, though it's often hard to see in the moment.

Motherhood also dismantles the myth of having it all figured out. It forces me to confront my limitations, to prioritize self-care. Before Luke, I rarely allowed myself to prioritize self-care. Motherhood teaches me that I can't pour from an empty cup. It's a lesson in grace, in understanding that vulnerability is strength.

This transforms my work life. I'm more attuned to colleagues' needs, learn to set boundaries, and prioritize effectively. My work life is more balanced and fulfilling. My journey has led me here. The past has lost its power over me. Luke's arrival was a sunrise, illuminating a new path. I carry the lessons learned, but no longer the weight of regret.

Luke, with his infectious giggle, reminds me of life's simple truths: joy in the ordinary, presence in the moment, the power of hope. He finds wonder in the smallest things, reminding me to appreciate the beauty around me. He inspires me to be a better person, to strive for compassion. He teaches me what it means to leave a legacy, not in grand gestures, but in everyday acts of love. Just watching him discover the world is a lesson in itself.

Every day, I strive to be the mother, wife, daughter, and friend I aspire to be. I'm a woman who embraces vulnerability, leads with empathy, shows up authentically, and believes in love's transformative power. Motherhood is refining me, revealing my true core. It has given me purpose, a deep love that fuels my every action.

Luke is my mentor, my legacy, and the reason I strive to be the best version of myself. In his eyes, I see the best version of myself, constantly evolving and growing, thanks to the profound love and unwavering hope motherhood has ignited within me. He is my greatest teacher, my inspiration, the reason I strive to make the world brighter. He has shown me the true meaning of legacy: not what you leave behind, but who you become along the way. My journey, with its twists and turns, the granted and ungranted wishes, has shown me that everything works out as it should, even when we can't see it at the time.

Lindsay Skredenske is a passionate advocate for St. Louis, driven by a deep commitment to community and empowerment. As Regional Director for Make-A-Wish Missouri & Kansas, she leads fundraising efforts, ensuring children with critical illnesses receive hope and joy. This mission resonates deeply with Lindsay, who navigated her own challenging path to motherhood, a journey that instilled in her the power of resilience and unwavering hope.

Previously, she founded City Block STL, a marketing agency that empowered 40+ organizations to amplify their community impact. Her entrepreneurial spirit and dedication to collaboration led her to build a successful company dedicated to strengthening the St. Louis community.

With nearly 15 years of experience in communications and development, Lindsay believes in the power of storytelling and collective action to build a brighter future for St. Louis. She is dedicated to fostering a vibrant and supportive community where everyone has the opportunity to thrive.

Please scan the QR code to connect with this author.

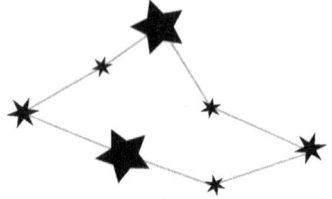

Lauren Kate Austin

The Strength From Within

There are no such things as fairy tales. For ten years I waited for someone to come save me. No one ever came. I had to save myself. When I was in the first grade, I remember standing at the top of the water slide ride called the Blow Out at Fiesta Texas. I stood there with a cast on my right wrist and waited for a couple of grown men to take on this slide. It went straight down. It was new to the park, and I couldn't wait. The men eventually chickened out and I stepped up for my turn as they would have to take the stairs back down. I looked at them as they stared back at me, and I crossed my broken arm over the other across my chest and flew down the slide.

That was the girl I was in childhood. I was a risk taker who played with the boys on co-ed sports teams. If something scared me, I would still do it. I thought I had such an exciting life in front of me. With that zest for life who knows what I could do with it!

Another path was taken. As I started to struggle with my weight, I not only knew I wasn't skinny like the other girls, but my body was just different. It was that self-realization that caused a huge change in my take on life. My self-confidence plummeted, and I was self-conscious in everything I wore, even the baggy catholic schoolgirl uniforms I wore to school. I didn't know much about eating disorders, but I always knew there could be ways to handle the food I ate. As I was struggling with volleyball in my junior year, my dad had a conversation with me and said that maybe if I lost weight, I could jump higher.

That was when it snapped in me. I had to lose weight. I went to the bathroom after and made myself throw up for the first time. I thought I would feel horrible, but instead, I felt a sense of relief. It was like everything was ok since I didn't technically eat that meal I had just swallowed. Now I know it was a sense of feeling "high."

At the age of seventeen, I was throwing up after most of my meals. I would be at home or at restaurants, go to an upstairs bathroom while everyone was eating lunch at school, and throw up. It was consuming my life immediately. I kept waiting for the weight to come off, but I never really lost any weight. I became addicted and couldn't stop.

This lasted ten years. I would go through cycles where I would be ok and not throw up but soon something would happen in my life that made me feel out of control and I was back in my cycle. The girl I once was or thought I could be was lost, hidden. She would stay hidden until one day it was enough.

My 4th year of being a 5th grade teacher (I was 27) in south Houston was difficult enough to keep my disorder at an all-time high. I was miserable at work. I had no personal life, no boyfriend, and felt too ugly to even date. I started to do the math. For ten years I had been bulimic. This was a secret only two people knew about. How could I have let it go on this long? I was just trying to lose weight in high school. Now it consumed me, and my day revolved around it. What was this life? I said, "No more." It had to change.

During what would be my last year as a teacher, I enrolled in a master's program at the University of Houston to continue my studies in Exercise Sciences. I was still an athlete at heart and dreamed of a career that involved sports, not teaching.

I felt like a fraud though. I could run a half marathon, but I also couldn't control my bulimia. It had to end! I decided after very minimal research I would train for a bodybuilding competition. I saw the Figure category. The physiques on those women were what I dreamed I could look like. That minimal research led me to a trainer at a gym near to my house and I called him immediately. He brought me in for a consultation and workout. After an intense session, I knew this was what I needed. I needed accountability and I needed that goal of a show.

Up until that point, I had always thought that working out was more important than what you ate, but Dewayne Malone very quickly changed that mindset. He gave me a meal plan to follow and if you ever meet Dewayne, you know that cheating is not an option for his clients. I never told him about my bulimia, worried he would fire me, but I was also determined to follow the plan. I ate everything on that plan every day and very quickly my body changed. A huge weight seemed to be lifting off my shoulders as I prepared my food every day and knew that every day I ate, the leaner I would get.

One day during a brutal workout, that I later dubbed mega death leg day, I told him I skipped my late-night protein shake. My old mindset was the less you eat the better. Dewayne got upset with me. He said, "Why would you do that? You are missing those calories, and your body needs them." It was at that moment that the switch finally flipped. Food is fuel, it is not the enemy. I am not saying it was an instantaneous fix for my disorder but that was my light switch moment. This led me to dive into competition training and I wanted to know everything. I needed to know everything because I was not ever going backward!

After I competed it was just the most amazing feeling. I looked at those pictures. It was more than just how I looked, but in that short amount of time how far I had come with my mindset. Something was re-igniting within me, and I was beginning to walk with my head up and shoulders back again.

One show down and I was ready for my next one. One day while on the cable seated row Dewayne asked me if I would come work for him. He is a very successful trainer and had too many clients. He knew I was unhappy teaching, and I enthusiastically agreed to work for him. That May, I packed up all my stuff from my classroom and left without looking back. It was the scariest thing I have ever done, but I felt like I was back. Doing the uncomfortable thing, challenging myself, I found myself again. Lauren was back in business.

My mentorship with Dewayne started in 2013 and has been ongoing since. I worked for him directly for two years before the next scary transition, going off fully on my own. During those two years, he allowed me to shadow him, run his business, sign new clients, get certified in nutrition, make meal plans, and see how it really is on the inside being a successful full-time personal trainer.

I was armed with the knowledge of closing clients, how to charge them, and how to run my day-to-day to maximize my time. It was not an easy thing, but I found a passion for training and helping others. On the gym floor standing over people while they pushed themselves to new limits is where I found my new place in life. It just fit. I knew that even if people didn't have my same disordered eating patterns, many people need a person to help them stay accountable and show up for them.

In just a few short years I was making six figures, a yearly amount of money I would long be hopeful to ever earn as a teacher. It was thanks to Dewayne. He led me through those years and allowed me to become my own version of a personal trainer.

Over these years I have trained many women for remarkable transformations. This included helping many women become professionals,

Pros, on the stage for fitness competitions. In 2018, I began to think about how nice it would be to have ladies who want to train for either a show or everyday life have a community of other women who are working toward similar goals. When you take on a hard goal, it can become difficult to stay focused as so many people in our everyday lives distract us from those goals. A group of women both online and in person would be a great way to help my ladies achieve their goals. ***Thus, the Boss Girls Brand was born***.

Boss Girls Brand started out with Boot camps and evolved into a community of women. I work to empower their lives through their fitness journey, taking control over their health. It really is a powerful move when you see a woman change. They have reached a place where enough is enough. When they are sick and tired of being sick and tired, you see the light switch moment. They are ready to take on not just the gym, but the world. Today, you can experience the Boss Girls Movement as the community grows on our website, Instagram, community calls, online workouts, and in-person confidence events.

No one is going to come save you. There isn't a rescue operation ready to come if you hit rock bottom. It must come from within **you** to make lasting change for the good of your life. With the right mentor and a life in fitness that centers around discipline, I was pulled back on my life's journey. When you arm yourself with the confidence you build in the gym, you'd be surprised at how much you change in your day-to-day life; with your career, family, and where you see yourself in the future.

Lauren Kate Austin is an entrepreneur from Houston, Texas and the founder of Boss Girls Brand, a brand dedicated to empowering women to embrace leadership and success. With professional training in, Exercise and Sports Sciences has built a dynamic career that combines innovation, determination, and a passion for helping women thrive.

Please scan the QR code to connect with this author.

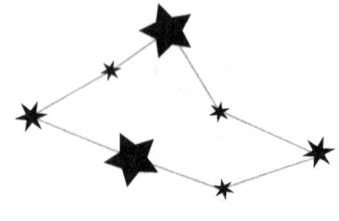

Nya Dorsey

A Life-Changing Encounter

If there's one thing that I've always stood by, it's that everything happens for a reason. And sometimes those moments that encompass that "everything" change the trajectory of our lives forever. Take it from Apostle Paul, who in one encounter with the Lord, went from persecutor to Prisoner of Christ Jesus. Even more, it was the ones the Lord placed in his path that helped him along the way.

Apostle Paul is considered one of the most influential figures in Christian history, with his God-inspired insights lifting, leading, and leaving a legacy amongst believers to this day. You may be quite surprised, however, to find out that before Paul hit the ground running for the Lord, he was famous for being murderous. Yes, Paul was a devout Pharisee constantly persecuting the children of God.

One fateful day as he was on his way to Damascus to arrest more disciples of the Lord, Paul was stopped in his tracks by a heavenly light and an unfamiliar voice. Just like that, Paul's life as he knew it was completely changed.

What does all of this have to do with anything? I promise you it will all make sense once I talk about a significant part of *my* personal journey—Maryville University. From the new friendships to the overwhelming sense of community, I learned so much about myself through my experiences there—some good, some not so good. In the end, I made it through.

As a communications major, I had the luxury of getting to know most of my professors closely during my undergraduate, and even beyond during my graduate studies. With our numbers, it was hard not to. I didn't fully grasp the power of those connections until 2020. I had just gotten back from spring break and received an email stating that all on-campus classes would be suspended for the remainder of the semester.

My life was suddenly changed. I was back in my childhood home, finishing up my bachelor's in my bedroom, sleeping for hours on end, and applying for jobs and apartments back in St. Louis. I was anxious, battling my own internal issues, and overall, just over it. This cycle kept repeating itself until the Lord told me to let it go. "Excuse me Lord…*let it go*?" It made no sense. How could I possibly "let it go," at a time like this? The world was shut down, and all I wanted was for things to go back to the way they were. Reluctantly I did. I let my present worries go. Life continued to move on, as it does.

It was March 2020. I was logging into LinkedIn when I heard a small "ding." I looked up and clicked my inbox notification. The message began, "Hi Nya—You were recommended to me by Rebecca Dorhman, a long-time respected friend of mine in the industry…"

My eyes widened. Throughout college they tell you about the importance of LinkedIn, but at the time, the only thing going through your mind is "…*sure*." Yet, here it was happening, from a connection through a *former* professor at that. I was overtaken by emotion. A bit more back and forth, a couple of writing samples, and one unorthodox interview on my mother's couch later, I started my journey at Fierce Creative Agency and have been there since.

It was April 2023. I was visiting the communications portfolio defense to support some of my fellow communication majors who were graduating that May. It was my first time seeing my former professors since the pandemic—one being Dr. Leilani Carver, a wonderful woman with a bright smile and the warmest heart. After the portfolio defense, she sent me a message on LinkedIn saying how good it was to see me. She followed up by saying that, with my master's, I could be a professor now. The thought of being a professor had crossed my mind here and there, but with that one sentence it seems the seed began to fully take root. As time went by, I didn't hear from Dr. Carver. I was worried that I had missed my timing. With a slightly heavy heart, I put it in the Lord's hands. As it always does, time went on.

Fast forward to July 2024. I was at a journalism summer camp we host for my job in Des Moines, Iowa. We were finally in for the night. Exhausted from the day, I stretched out in the bed checking my emails. I saw that I had a new message waiting for me from Dr. Carver. I flung open the LinkedIn app and clicked on the notification. It started, "Hi! I have a class I want you to teach this fall." I leaped out of the bed. This must be the time.

Rewind to Paul. There's a part of his story that I hadn't thought of before until my Pastor went through an exposition of Acts 9. After Paul encountered Jesus on the Damascus Road, he was left blind for three days. The Lord then speaks to a believer in Damascus named Ananias in a vision, telling him to go and find Paul to lay hands on him and pray for him so that he might see again. As you can expect, Ananias hesitated a bit. You and I might too if the Lord asked us to go and pray for someone who is known to persecute people like you. In his obedience, Ananias went and found Paul and prayed for him. The Bible says that something as scales fell off Paul's eyes. He could see again. From that moment on, he began preaching boldly in the name of Jesus.

What is there to say about Apostle Paul? A lot. One of the main things being that he did *not* expect his life to change the way it did on the Damascus Road. The Lord set him on a new path. Sometimes we don't understand what's going on in our lives. Sometimes we have a vision of how it's supposed to be. Then one day, one encounter changes it all. Paul had a constellation, which was comprised of a lot of people who were terrified of him. One star he didn't account for, though, was the True North Star, which is Jesus Christ, who would lead and guide him exactly where he needed to be...where he was **chosen to be.**

How interesting that it would be those same terrified believers who in his time of need would come and rescue *him* from being persecuted (Acts 9:24-25). I can think on my experiences and see the same revelations.

I didn't know that the same Professor Dohrman whom I met during my freshman year of college would be the same one who would recommend me for my first job. Back then, I didn't know that I would *yet* be connected to her, getting invaluable insights on coming into my own as a professor.

I didn't know that the same Dr. Carver from my college career would be the same one leading and lifting me through my higher-education career. I couldn't see at the time that she would be helping me set up my classes with her kind heart and her bright, welcoming smile.

When I started at Fierce, I had no idea that my boss, Kate Manfull, who interviewed me on my mother's couch, would be the same one ecstatic about my adjunct professor role, immediately working out a schedule so that I could pursue it with comfort. I couldn't have told you that she would be the same one who offered to sponsor me for **this** book you're reading now, because she knew of my desire and efforts to be an author.

We never know who God will place in our lives, and the ultimate blessings that they can become in our time our need. Nothing is happenstance in God. Whether you're guided or someone is guided toward you. That's why we must consider every connection we stumble upon a divine appointment from God to add to our constellations, even if we're unsure of it in the moment.

As I reflect on my journey and those who have led and lifted me, it would be very remiss of me to not talk about my spiritual walk with Christ. Not only does the Lord constantly lead and lift me through this life, but He has also placed some phenomenal mentors in my constellation to help build **me** up as a woman of God.

My grandmother, Barbara Cross, has risen time and time again despite many hardships and trials. Her joy has carried her through this life, and her generosity and kindness have moved me in mine.

My mother, Nathasia Dorsey, is a lioness who refuses to back down. She has taught me resilience; she has taught me strength. Most importantly, she has taught me to never give up on God. Even when the situation looks impossible, we know that our God is faithful and will never fail.

My First Lady, Dr. Leticia Parks, is the epitome of beauty and grace. She is a prayer warrior, who can cut to the root of a matter and bind up any wounds so tenderly at the same time. I'm grateful for the love that she has given me, and the wisdom to remember that the most beautiful part of myself is the Spirit of God within me (1 Peter 3:3-4).

My Pastor, Dr. Chris A. Parks, is an anointed man of God who consistently lives by the word and challenges our church daily to do the same. If you had told me five years ago that my Damascus Road experience would lead me here, experiencing the breakthrough that I've experienced while being under his leadership, I would have laughed in your face. Through the divine power of God, and one divine encounter, here I am.

My Pastor spoke to me about my legacy in 2021. He said, "Nya you must think about your legacy…you have a whole world to impact for the glory of God." At that time, I was freshly going through the deliverance process. Leaving a legacy was the last thing on my mind. He encouraged and prayed for me like Paul, to have the scales fall from my eyes to **see** God's will for my life, to **embrace** my destiny, and to **know** that God is already fulfilling it all.

If we know that the people we encounter become a part of our constellation, maybe it's not hard to see how we can move to lead and lift them *now* for their future—even if our encounter is for a short moment. We may not know what all will happen in our lives, but we know that there will be lasting impacts for whatever it is. Why not be intentional about each and every moment?

If I had to leave something as a legacy, it would be this simple, overwhelming *truth*—When God moves, He changes lives. **Forever.** I'm living proof of that. Now that these words are a part of your constellation, so are *you*.

May the Lord bring divine connections into your life to lead you, lift you, and be a part of your legacy. May you, in turn, lead, and lift those around you in love. And may all the moments you encounter bring you exactly to where you need to be in Christ, now and forever more.

Nya Dorsey is a project manager at Fierce Creative Agency, handling day-to-day client contact and providing creative solutions to complex challenges. Passionate about sharing meaningful messages, Nya also serves as an Adjunct Professor of Public Speaking at Maryville University of St. Louis, sharing her expertise with aspiring communicators.

Beyond work, Nya enjoys exploring new restaurants, flexing her artistic muscles through painting and drawing, and cherishing quality time with family. Rooted and driven by her faith, Nya is grateful for her relationship with God, which inspires her to strive for excellence in all aspects of her life.

Please scan the QR code to connect with this author.

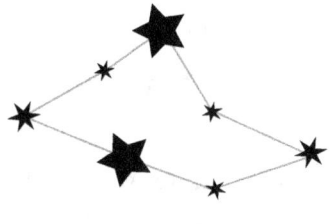

Bea Doerr

Grateful

I was sitting in our company's first meeting of the year, and our leadership had decided to play a game. They wanted to put the 2024 rattled year behind and start on a new foot with forward thinking. A few questions were displayed on a screen, and we all took turns plucking two phrases from the nine to speak about. I came in a little late to the game with dropping of Kay, my daughter, after a 3-week hiatus with her. The holidays and the infamous St. Louis snowstorm kept us at home base for almost a week. Needless to say, she had a tough time letting go of my leg when I dropped her off at school. I had a ton of mom guilt, so my heart and I stayed with her until it was ok to leave.

I pulled my chair in while people were already going around the room speaking about their top phrases. I was drawn to the "What Are You Grateful For?" topic. I don't know why, but my tears already started dancing out of my eyes. Maybe it was the hard time I was having dropping off Kay, but my family was already in my head. I like my regimen schedule, but I was having a difficult time pulling away from home. The old saying, "There's No Place Like Home" flashed multiple times in my head.

Then, everyone looked at me, "Grateful". Sounds cheesy but I am more grateful for my family than ever. I was taken back to when I graduated from Illinois State University and started my photojournalism career only to be knocked around with layoffs, setbacks and no future stability. I tried to stay in "it" because I loved my career. I had embarked on having a studio, contract work with various companies, wedding photography, and then side jobs with school photography. By 2014 it was coming to an end. I came back to the "Lou" after more than twenty years of being gone. I had come home and pursued a new career. In 2018, I found the love of my life and married. Fast forward to 2020, we went through the IVF process, and by faith in the Lord we welcomed Kayleigh Elizabeth Doerr on March 11, 2021. Grateful! Neither I nor my love, Kris Doerr, would have imagined we would have a healthy and happy child. She gives us a daily light in our lives and some feisty challenges, but we are grateful to have our little being.

I sit here typing away and my husband is already in deep slumber. I'm grateful for Kris because he really is my balance in life. We are not perfect or profess it. We have our battles like everyone else but also know we are grateful to have each other at the end of the day. Until Kris came along, I never imagined being married, let alone having a family. We both said our "I Do's" in an earlier life before we met each other, just not to our soulmates. We have each other's backs and above all, our faith. Yes, we continue to be tested as all are. I even tried to set him up with numerous friends before he became the one for me. I just thought he was and is such a tremendous human being. One day, I could not imagine being without him for better or for worse. Grateful.

As I sat in church this past Sunday, the communications director wanted to honor a fourth-floor church member. The status is not only a member coming to church, but someone who participates beyond the average churchgoer. She came up to the stage for a little ceremony celebrating the top floor and I noticed "Grateful" on her shirt. This really grounded me. I have gone through many chapters from thinking my career was going to be a photojournalist only to end up unexpectedly laid-off multiple times. I eventually opened my own photography studio to be in control of my own destiny. I ran out of contracts and had to work a part-time job to make ends meet. I ended up in Iowa for a year after landing an operations position with a school picture company thinking I would learn, grow, and become a District Manager. I found out the company had plans for my staying in Iowa since I was doing "such a good job." With these transitions, I had to lean on faith. I was actually roaming the streets when I was laid off the first time dropping resumes off. I spent time in the unemployment office daily to fill out forms to collect. I'm not sure how I kept my calm state but prayed many times for God to lead me on a path. I'm grateful to God. Without *Him* I would not be back in St. Louis, surrounded by family, married, with my baby girl and our little puppy "Tipsy".

I think the more we live life to the fullest, we stumble upon hard lessons, especially if we are putting ourselves out there completely and fully. I have such a deep gratitude for the challenges I have faced, because without those I would not be grateful for what I have today. Do not get me wrong. I am still a work in progress and have to step back to look at life in a less granular way. By this, I mean, not so ingrained in the things I do not have and embracing what I do have.

Since returning to St. Louis in 2014 I have continually experienced many networking groups. I used to be an avid bicyclist and was a part of a few biking groups. It really saved me because I did not know anyone and wanted to socialize outside of work and family. I'm grateful for this group because I had great friendships and experiences that opened doors to other adventures and social events.

I am grateful for the networking community we have in St. Louis, for which I probably would not be, so humbly, a part of this book. A few years ago, when I joined the company, I had received my business cards and did a quick overview of the front and back. On the back, the mission statement read "Help Businesses Succeed So Communities Prosper." At the time, it did not really resonate with me. I started going to every event and scheduling as many coffees, lunches and attending happy hours as much as possible. This was a step up from my four hundred cold calls a week, while pregnant during the pandemic. I started cultivating relationships and really connected with individuals. I am so blessed and grateful for the network and continuing the journey.

Grateful is a word we all probably forget about in our daily grind. God pulls me back sometimes when I get off track. I think I will write the word on a Post-it and place it around the house, in my car, at the office, and perhaps on my head. It's such a powerful word and something we could all pause and reflect on. What are you Grateful for?

Born and raised in St. Louis, Bea played volleyball for Illinois State University. She graduated with a bachelor's in arts and sciences and a Minor in Photography. She started as a photojournalist for a Newspaper in Central Illinois and freelanced throughout the country including The Associated Press and The St. Louis Post-Dispatch. Bea became a contract photographer and had her own studio. She moved to Iowa to become the Photography and Operations Manager for the number one family-owned picture studios. In 2014, she started a new adventure and switched gears into the sales and marketing consulting role. After a few years in the St. Louis market, she is now a Certified Business Performance Advisor. She resides in South County and adores her little 3-year-old Kayleigh and amazing husband Kris. She is happy to be back home and surrounded by all her family and fur baby, Tipsy. Grateful!

Please scan the QR code to connect with this author.

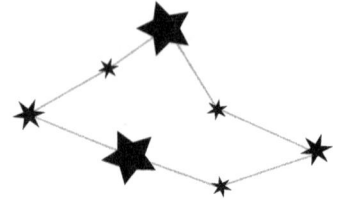

Lauren Pronger

Why the Heck Not?

From the moment I was six years old, my life was defined by a single question: *Why not?* When my father was diagnosed with stage four colon cancer, a disease that could have brought fear and despair into our family, he instead turned to living boldly. He refused to see his diagnosis as an end. Instead, it was a beginning—a call to immerse himself in the beauty of life and the possibilities of healing. Together, we began exploring the world, not just for its sights but for its lessons.

As a young girl, I found myself learning about meditation, acupuncture, deep detoxes, culinary medicine, and countless other holistic healing modalities as we traveled. While I could not have fully understood it at the time, those early experiences planted the seeds for what would become the foundation of my life's purpose: the pursuit of transformative wellness and creating a space for others to experience the same.

My Father: My Mentor, My Angel

My father was so much more than a parent; he was my greatest mentor, my best friend, and my most steadfast cheerleader. He lived his life with humility, gratitude, and an unshakable belief in the power of creating something meaningful—whether it was building a legacy, nurturing his family, or helping others heal.

He taught me to approach life with intention, curiosity, and joy. He was the kind of man who found beauty and purpose in every moment, whether it was sitting down for a meal, spending time in nature, or learning something new. Through his actions, he showed me how to create a life worth celebrating, one that leaves a lasting mark on the world.

One of his most profound lessons was the importance of resilience—not in fighting against life, but in embracing it fully. He showed me that challenges are not roadblocks; they are opportunities for growth. His unwavering positivity shaped me in ways I am still uncovering.

Even now, I feel his guidance every day. My father had an incredible way of opening the right doors and closing the ones that were not meant for me. When he was here on Earth, he placed opportunities in my path that shaped my journey. And now, from heaven, he continues to be my strategic angel, nudging me toward the people, experiences, and lessons that are meant for me.

Burnout to Brilliance: My Turning Point

In 2011, my life felt like it was crumbling. My husband Chris had suffered a career-ending injury in the NHL, one that left us navigating the mental health obstacles that often accompany severe and repeated concussions from his 20 years of play. Together, we faced the emotional and psychological aftermath of those injuries, working through them as a couple and rebuilding our resilience as a team. Around the same time, my father had a debilitating stroke, and my mother was diagnosed with breast cancer. I was a mother of three young children, trying to hold everything together while the weight of these crises threatened to consume me.

I was burned out in every sense of the word—physically, emotionally, and spiritually. I felt like I was running on fumes, trying to be everything to everyone while neglecting my own health and well-being. It was in this storm of adversity that I realized something had to change.

I began to rebuild myself, piece by piece. I turned to the lessons my father had taught me—about living with intention, prioritizing wellness, and finding strength in vulnerability. I began to explore holistic healing modalities, from meditation and breathwork to nutrition and movement. I prioritized sleep, balance, and mindfulness, carving out time to care for my own body and spirit.

This journey from burnout to brilliance was not a quick fix, but a transformation. It ignited a fire in me to not only heal myself but to help others do the same. This was the moment when I started to see the vision for what would eventually become SUPERWELL.

Building a Life on Purpose

When I founded Well Inspired Travels in 2018, I had a clear vision. I wanted to create more than a luxury travel agency. I wanted to design journeys that prioritized healing and transformation, combining the best of the world's wellness destinations with personalized, intentional experiences. From advanced diagnostics to spa therapies, from spiritual retreats to culinary adventures, each itinerary was crafted with one goal in mind: helping clients feel their absolute best.

As the business grew, Chris joined me, bringing his perspective as a professional athlete to the table. Together, we built a business that not only planned incredible trips but also transformed lives. Clients were not just traveling for leisure; they were discovering themselves, resetting their health, and uncovering new possibilities for their well-being.

Even as Well Inspired Travels became a movement, I knew my journey did not stop there. I realized that helping people become *well* was not enough. I wanted to help them become SUPERWELL. After all, why stop at good when you can strive for great? Why the heck not?

From Well to SUPERWELL

SUPERWELL is more than a lifestyle. It is a mindset. It is about going beyond wellness to achieve vitality, resilience, and joy. It is about living with intention and showing up as the best version of yourself every day—physically, emotionally, and spiritually.

The SUPERWELL Living Community grew out of my passion to share this philosophy. Central to it are the Eight Pillars of the SUPERWELL Living Method: Well-Aging, Optimal Sleep, Balanced Flow, Emotional Wellness, Nature Connection, Nourishing Nutrition, BioRhythm and Mindfulness, and Soulful Connection. These pillars provide a comprehensive framework, guiding individuals to not only heal but thrive. They ensure every facet of life—from physical health to emotional and spiritual alignment—is supported and nurtured.

Drawing from my certifications as a board-certified holistic practitioner, certified contrast therapy guide, breathwork specialist, and meditation guide, as well as my studies at the Institute of Integrative Nutrition, I developed this method to address the full spectrum of well-being.

Through SUPERWELL, I teach people how to integrate tools like contrast therapy, red light therapy, biohacking, grounding, and mindful nutrition into their daily lives. More than that, I show them how to create balance, how to prioritize joy, and how to embrace their personal power.

Every day when I wake up, I remind myself of the mantra that has guided me since I was a little girl: *I am the well, striving to be SUPERWELL. Why the heck not?* This mantra is at the heart of everything I do. It is a reminder that we are all on a journey and that I am here as a guide for those walking the same path.

What fuels SUPERWELL, however, is not just the science-backed practices—it is the community. It is the women and men who show up every day to share their stories, celebrate their victories, and support one another through their struggles. Together, we embody the idea that strong is the new beautiful and that wellness is a lifelong journey.

Leading by Example

Leadership is not about telling people what to do; it is about showing them what is possible. For me, that has meant living by the principles I teach. It has meant being open about my own journey—the moments of burnout, the challenges of motherhood, and the small victories that come from showing up for myself every day. Through vulnerability, I have built connection. And through connection, I have found my legacy.

A Legacy of Leadership and Inspiration

What does it mean to leave a legacy? For me, it means creating something that outlives me—not in the form of a building or a business, but in the lives I have touched and the seeds I have planted. It means knowing that the people I have worked with, whether through Well Inspired Travels or SUPERWELL, will carry a piece of this journey with them.

It is the client who tells me they rediscovered their confidence after a SUPERWELL retreat. It is the mother who decides to prioritize her own health for the first time in years. It is the friend who overcomes their fears because they saw me step into mine first. These moments are my legacy, and they remind me why this work matters.

Today, as I reflect on this journey—from that six-year-old girl learning about holistic healing with her father to the woman I am now—I feel overwhelming gratitude. Gratitude for the lessons I have learned, the people I have met, and the opportunities I have had to make an impact. None of us know how much time we have, but we do know we have today. Today is enough. It is enough to show love, make an impact, and leave the world better than we found it. To anyone reading this: If you are waiting for the right moment to chase your dreams, to take care of yourself, or to live boldly, let me remind you—why the heck not?

As I continue building the SUPERWELL Living Community, my focus remains the same: helping people move from simply existing to thriving. Whether it is through a retreat, a digital course, or a conversation, I want to leave people better than I found them. At the end of the day, legacy is not about perfection. It is about the lives we touch, the inspiration we spark, and the love we leave behind.

My father taught me that at six years old. Now, I am teaching it to the world, with him guiding me every step of the way—from Earth and from Heaven.

Lauren Pronger is a visionary leader in wellness and transformative travel, whose journey began at the age of six when she was first introduced to holistic healing while traveling with her father. As the founder of Well Inspired Travels, Lauren curates luxury wellness experiences that nourish the mind, body, and spirit. She is also the creator of SUPERWELL Living, a movement dedicated to guiding individuals from *burnout to brilliance* through her eight-pillar method. With 10 certifications across multiple health and wellness disciplines—including holistic nutrition, meditation, breathwork, and contrast therapy—Lauren continues to push the boundaries of optimal living. Her lifelong mantra *"I am the well, striving to be SUPERWELL. Why the heck not?"* reflects her unwavering passion for elevating others. Through her work, she is building a legacy of empowerment, helping others reclaim their vitality and embrace a life of purpose, wellness, and resilience.

Please scan the QR code to connect with this author.

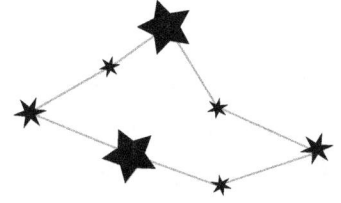

Jacqueline Duty

I Don't Know

*"The more I know, the more I know I **don't** know."*

The words of one of my favorite mentors rang through my ears long after he passed away. It was such a profound statement that came at a crucial time in my life. It can be easy when you are in the early phase of your career to move boldly with confidence, even arrogance, as you strive to prove yourself in the business world. Eric MacDougall invested so many years in the newspaper industry traveling around the country to train salespeople in advertising sales with a focus on the automotive industry.

He shared many key tips for success in the media industry, but the most important lesson he shared was the day he said how we should never stop learning. "The more I know, the more I know, I **don't** know." He was a master at the dramatic pause when delivering a compelling message. This statement stuck. I learned to always maintain the heart of a student. As soon as we think we have mastered an area, things can change. Industries shift and there is always somebody who knows more than us in any given area. If we are really paying attention, we can learn from every person we meet. Identifying strong coaches and mentors can be the fuel you need to get to the next area of your life.

Leading with Integrity

Growing up, I was an athlete trying to perform at the highest levels in every sport. It was important to me to understand the dynamics of each sport that was available. I loved playing soccer and played with some of the best over a 12-year period. I also enjoyed investing my time in softball, volleyball, basketball, track, and cross country. Every evening in the summer, I could be found playing football on the streets with the neighborhood kids until the lights came on. I took lessons in tennis, archery, and any sport offering a weekly camp. I spent hours consuming the performances of my heroes like Jackie Joyner Kersee and Ozzie Smith. I felt there were always so many lessons to learn from the top-performing athletes in all sports.

It was a surreal moment when I found myself in business with a child-hood hero who played for the St. Louis Cardinals. A friend called me one day and said to meet her for lunch and to meet Todd Stottlemyre. He was in town building a mobile company and looking for business partners. This would launch the next several years of my building another business. The people I met were incredible. Every week we would gather to train, learn systems, and focus on building a mindset for success. Todd Stottlemyre became the greatest coach I would have. I always valued the power of having a great coach in sports. I made sure I sought out strong mentors in business. It never occurred to me to have a coach in life to ensure I was analyzing every area for success. Todd would mention how we become the average of the five people we spend the most time with. Building a team of champions created accountability that placed focus on results. I could write a book just on the lessons Todd has taught through his training program. His level of integrity and passion to help train champions is truly inspiring. After a devastating house fire that would change my life, Todd called and walked me through his 180-degree mindset training. It was exactly what I needed to keep moving forward after a tragedy that could have derailed my life. I will forever be grateful for his coaching, mentoring, and friendship.

Lifting In Love

Fear rang through my heart as I hung up the phone in 2022. I just received news that my husband was getting transported to ICU and there was a 15% chance that he would live through the night. I felt like my world was crumbling. After 22 years of marriage, it was hard to think of how different life would be as a widow. After I called our parents, I sat on my sofa staring at the wall. Who could I call? It was 1:00 in the morning and I had never felt more alone. I wasn't allowed to see my husband in the hospital because of restrictions from the pandemic as hospitals were once again being filled to capacity. The doctor informed me that they were trying to get him airlifted to another hospital, but no beds were available in any hospital in St. Louis. They didn't think they had the capacity to help him. It was imperative that he get to an ICU unit that could help. There was nothing I could do except pray.

I called my pastors. When you need a team of prayer warriors to surround you, you reach out to the best. I was so thankful to have Pastor Myles and Valerie Holmes on my side. They answered the call and immediately rallied the troops. The week that followed can only be described as the miracle of a healing God. He was placed in a top hospital in St. Louis the next day. Then I was told he would be in the hospital for several weeks. He might be able to get out of ICU in one to two weeks. I watched him walk out of the hospital seven days later. Only God can do that.

At one of the lowest moments of my life, my pastors were there. No judgment; just love. I have found in life that when tragedy strikes, people are very quick to make assumptions. They can be completely inaccurate, but human nature can place our biases, filters, and judgments at the forefront of communication. Be kind, always. You never know what a person can be going through. Surround yourself with people who will love you with no judgment and walk with you through the chaos that life can deliver unexpectedly. I'm very thankful for my pastors who have loved us even when we weren't always loveable.

Leaving a Legacy of Honor and Loyalty

It's impossible to talk about mentors and leaving a legacy without highlighting the incredible lessons learned from my most impactful mentor—my dad.

From the beginning, my dad set the tone that every situation should be approached with faith in God. As long as I can remember, he has carved a path to move forward through life's biggest challenges with a heart of faith, gratitude, and prayer.

I want to take time to honor all the wisdom he has been able to share with me. I even interviewed him to try to gather the most impactful information. I could write a book just on those lessons. I certainly don't have the space to cover it all here. The most prominent subject that he highlighted was about family. Friends can come and go. Jobs can be eliminated or removed. Hobbies and passions can change over time. Family remains. At the end of our life, we won't be looking at the trophies on the wall or the "stuff" that felt so important when we bought them. Hopefully, we will be surrounded by the people who mean the most as we share stories that can carry from generation to generation.

Many hours have been invested in sharing stories about family members. I would hear excitement as he shared about my Great-Grandpa as a soldier in World War I. I would laugh with joy when he shared moments on the farm with my grandparents. Through it all, I felt the emotions of compassion, respect, and love towards the legacy they established as they fought to give everything they had for the family. The words that ring through the generations are "God first, then family, then everything else."

My parents are the most loving people who have been a demonstration of how people are the most important things on this side of eternity. Family is the cornerstone of building a legacy that lasts. Through your family, your story continues and will be etched on the hearts of those who carry your name forward. It's within these relationships that the true measure of a life well lived is preserved and celebrated.

Life can deliver circumstances that hit like a truck. It has the potential to knock you completely off course from the plans you carefully crafted. How you respond to these circumstances will define all of your "tomorrows." People can come to you in desperation to seek help in their life-altering moments. Sometimes, the best thing you can do is shrug your shoulders and say, "I don't know…but we will figure it out together."

Jacqueline Duty is a Chilean artist, author, speaker, and marketing consultant. She invested a twenty-year career in corporate media working for metropolitan newspapers, magazines, radio stations, television, and digital media. She launched her digital marketing agency and online media company to help businesses tell their story.

She serves as the Commissioner of Communication for the National Memorial of Military Ascent. Helping to launch the Grafton Art Gallery, she works with groups across the region to promote art. Jacqueline sells her art, photography, and books to highlight her Hispanic heritage.

She serves many civic organizations and enjoys spending time with her husband Steve and two sons, Tyler and Trevor.

Jacqueline remains dedicated to helping people pursue their purpose and achieve success. She lives by her mantra: "When the fire inside of you burns greater than the fires around you, you are positioned to pursue purpose. Restore brokenness, heal, and honor the journey."

Please scan the QR code to connect with this author.

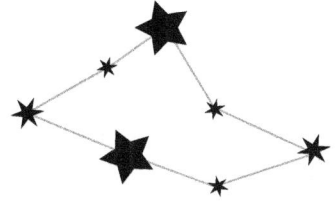

Annie Sorensen

The Importance of Your Personal Village

It was a crisp, fall day when I got the phone call that I had breast cancer. I was carrying my 18-month-old son on my hip and watching my 3-year-old daughter skip around a tree on the property outside of her preschool. I had just picked her up and we had about an hour and a half left of our afternoon before we had to pick up my eldest daughter from kindergarten. I sat in my minivan after hanging up with the doctor, buried my face in my hands, and cried.

The days and weeks that followed were full of tests, cold laboratory tables, and scary conversations with surgeons. During that time, I repeatedly became aware of how much I was being held and supported by the community of women around me. I had built a village I didn't have any plans of ever needing myself, yet there they were, and my personal and professional lives were never the same.

I graduated college with a business administration degree in Management Information Systems. I'm a stereotypical oldest child. I thought I could do everything myself. I wanted to accomplish the world and always got what I wanted.

I held a VP role in my sorority, was accepted into a global business fraternity, and volunteered with multiple charity organizations in college. I found a new job easily every summer, including a wonderful internship in the IT department of a large construction company the summer before my senior year. By the following November, I had a permanent job offer from that company and another offer from a large medical software company in the Kansas City area. I took the medical software company job and moved to Kansas City with a car full of my possessions and one friend.

I got to work. I willingly worked over fifty hours per week, while also investing in multiple side hustles. Network marketing, real estate, blogging, and social media consulting; I did it all and I did it well. I was a one-woman, super show! I was thriving, and I was doing it all on my own.

I worked in support and engineering roles at that company, and after seven years decided to resign and take another path. I left behind the structure and prestige of a corporate job and started working full-time on my previously part-time hustles. I got my real estate license, investing in and remodeling a few properties. I also started writing more and landed several large freelance writing gigs. I volunteered weekly at our local library.

You can probably guess where this is going. A high-accomplishing woman who can do it all on her own and only focuses on herself? Surely there is a crash coming! Crash I did. A series of mistakes left me lost and alone, wracked with anxiety and diminishing self-worth. No one was there to notice. There is an old saying about the only two guarantees in life being death and taxes. I want to suggest a more modern version of that saying: the only two guarantees in life are that you will struggle, and that others around you will too.

My first mistake during my career was thinking I could do everything alone. I placed no value in building and maintaining a support system. This mistake I was able to push through for a while.

My second mistake was a series of missteps related to a lack of planning.

I left my corporate job without a solid framework for how I would structure my day around the businesses I had started, therefore causing me to float through my days without clear goals. This decreased my productivity and left me feeling directionless.

I agreed to be a stay-at-home parent without any self-reflection on if that was what I wanted. I was anxious, guilt-ridden, and confused.

I allowed my side hustles to slip away one by one as the demands of my family increased.

I never reached out to anyone who was in a similar situation for advice, support, and love.

It was this second series of mistakes that took me out, and I wasted a lot of time of the one and precious life I've been given. What I began to identify during this time was that I had no peers left in the corporate world, nor any peers with young children, nor any peers working freelance while attempting to balance a young family. I had no peers, period. Where were my people? Why didn't I have any people?! How did I end up here? Who was I becoming? I certainly wasn't the type-A, high-achieving, hard-working woman I was in my 20's. I didn't even have a fancy title anymore. If someone asked me what I did for a living, I was unable to clearly answer the question. I had failed to define what I was doing; therefore, I ended up doing nothing. I was lost with no one in my life who could hunt me down and bring me back.

What finally began to turn my tides was connecting with a built-in support system. Mine happened to be with the parents and staff at my children's preschool. Some of these women were working moms, some were stay-at-home moms, but what they all had in common was that they could relate.

This group of women understood when I couldn't really answer their questions about what I did for a living. They understood feeling lost in your career because you took a few pivots and suddenly didn't recognize where you were anymore. They understood all of it. They picked me up, opened my eyes to the power of having a supportive, encouraging village, and I was forever changed.

What did all these women have in common? They had a village of people who understood their personal situations and supported them. That personal support allowed their professional careers to take off in new and thrilling ways. They showed me with their actions how to build and maintain a support system. They taught me how to lift up the women around me. They taught me that what makes a strong woman stronger, is other strong women. They proved to me that lifting women up raises the tide for everyone.

We all are going to pivot, whether it is a proactive choice or something unexpectedly thrust upon us. Some pivots are purposeful, intentional, exciting, and planned. Others are not. Career pivots can be freeing and fulfilling! We might be able to do things alone for a while, and we might even succeed in doing so. At some point, we will run into an obstacle.

This is the message I wish I could go back and tell my 25-year-old self. We can't let those obstacles keep us from moving forward. We can't let them drown us, never sharing our situations or asking for help.

When my first child was born, an out-of-town friend sent flowers. Lovely! But not helpful. By the time our third was born, I had a village, and they showed up. We had multiple meals delivered that lasted for weeks. A friend cleaned my kitchen and did my laundry while I recovered and bonded with our new baby. My boss in my new role at church told me to not dare call her for at least eight weeks "or else."

Shortly after I returned to work, I applied for a leadership position within my team. I sat down with my boss to discuss it a couple of weeks later and she told me she was not going to give me that position because it was too low for me. She lifted me up when she said I should aim higher.

I was newly post-partum with three young children yet felt confident about my future career options. I could provide value to the marketplace. Don't let anyone tell you that personal connections and professional connections are separate. Your professional self is part of you, the person. That person has a personal life. I soon set aside time every day to lift up women around me, the way that the preschool community taught me to do. Without knowing it, I was building a village that would support me when I needed it.

Build the village, even if you don't yet need it. Pour into it, then, when needed, it will pour into you. Remember that it's not a matter of if you will struggle, but when. By the time of my cancer diagnosis, when everything was suddenly not okay, I was surrounded with love and support. My personal life and my professional life could not have been in better hands. I emerged from that chapter in my life stronger and more determined than ever.

How do you build your all-in-one, professional and personal village? One tiny act at a time. Focusing on serving those around you will get you the biggest bang for your buck. It will develop relationships in your lives that carry you always.

Lifting others up could be an act of service, it could be simple communication. It could be a hard conversation. It could be encouragement. It always includes sharing and being vulnerable. You can lift someone up in a personal way, which will affect their professional life. You could also lift someone up in a professional way that affects their personal life. Get into the habit of support. It's a muscle, you must use it regularly to keep it strong.

Your personal life and your professional life will be happier and more successful when you do. You can control who you lift up when they need it, but you cannot necessarily control who lifts you when you need it. Lifted someone and they were not there to lift you? Perhaps a reevaluation of that relationship is needed.

Lift those up around you to make your village the strongest it can be. Never discount the immense value of small actions, repeated consistently. Lift up your village with encouraging words, a listening ear, or just being present. Lift them with texts, gifts, and hugs. Introduce them to your recruiter friend. Encourage them to start posting on TikTok, because you know they're scared to, but have always wanted to do it. Tell them you're watching their baby for the afternoon so they can rest, or work on their resume, or meet that new client at the coffee shop. Put the date in your calendar of when their new job starts, so you can send them a confetti-popping congratulatory text, or so you can get a celebratory drink with them after their first successful week. Put the date in your calendar of the day their brother died, so you can check in. Email them the news article you ran into about that business book you chatted about last week.

However you choose to do it, do it often. Your village will make it through those inevitable life and career pivots faster, stronger, and healthier when you do. Their support for you will be there in return. Always remember how these seemingly small acts of lifting others add up. Trust me, I've experienced it. Lean into it all, and you will be ready for whatever life throws your way.

Was my cancer journey hard, harder than anything I had ever gone through, regardless of the people around me? Yes, absolutely. What made all the difference was how strong I was when I came out the other side, when I had a team of powerhouse women encouraging, listening, guiding, and loving on me and my family. I would not be where I am today – more than six years cancer-free, with a job I love and going after my dream of being a full-time writer and novelist – if it weren't for each and every one of them.

Annie Sorensen is a freelance writer, children's book author, and aspiring novelist. Her first published book, A Boy Named Love, is the result of a successful Kickstarter campaign that ran in December 2014.

After spending most of her 20s in software engineering, Annie left the corporate world to focus on various business interests and her growing family. She has experience in real estate, social media, investing, consulting, and more. She currently works in business operations at one of the largest churches in the country.

Annie loves to read, entertain friends, travel, and hike. She lives in the Kansas City area with her husband and three kids. You can connect with her on TikTok. Please don't message her when the Chiefs are playing.

Please scan the QR code to connect with this author.

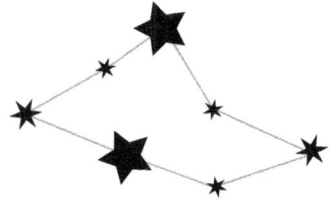

Kate Wilkins

Small Touches & Community Building

I sat in a familiar chair tracing my finger back and forth along the ridges of my armrest. I was in a room I'd become greatly acquainted with and a chair I'd grown fond of since starting at my new school. As my finger ran wild, I shared my most recent reason for requesting guidance from my favorite advisor. She listened to me and nodded her head understandingly. All her advice began by validating the gravity of my current teenage situation. Then, she'd share an open-ended anecdote that was shockingly similar to my own dilemma. None of her advice was particularly earth-shattering, but she'd been at the school for some time and was clearly experienced in the stresses of teenagers at a college preparatory school. The painful part about her guidance was that she never quite solved my problems for me. Instead, she'd lay out facts of the situation, point me in the right direction, and let me find my way to the answer on my own. It didn't matter how long it took me to arrive at a decision, she'd wait for me to get to the answer in my own time.

Learning how to make the right choices for myself when faced with tough decisions was one of my favorite lessons she taught me. Her office provided a safe space to weigh my options which gave me confidence in my decisions and articulating my thought processes. When I made my decisions, I felt secure in them. Cultivating this confidence in my decision-making skills was setting me up for success in all areas of my life, even if I didn't know it at the time.

Years later, as I reflect on our dynamic, I've learned to give others the space to make their own choices. I can offer advice or my perspective, but I cannot force anyone to make a decision. People will make decisions based on their own timeline and personal experiences. Once the knowledge and wisdom has been shared, it is up to the mentee to determine how they want to use it.

Flash forward a few years. I'm sitting on the ground floor of my university's Arts and Science building, listening to a new friend as she thinks out loud. She was a year above in college, and we shared one of the same majors. We intended to use this time to study for an upcoming statistics exam. In this moment, I don't remind her. Her thoughts flow out of her and I'm a rapt audience. She's game-planning her semester: what classes she needs to take, what clubs she's planning on joining, and what jobs or research options to investigate. As I listened to her rattling off opportunities I had never heard of or even considered before, all I could think to myself was "I want to do all of that." I meant it.

By the end of the semester, we were co-chairs in our sorority. I joined more clubs and asked her advice on so many of my endeavors. Her advice was generally delivered with just the right mixture of encouragement and authenticity that felt particularly powerful to me. Of course, we didn't agree on everything. What worked for her often didn't work for me. Still, getting the perspective of someone who'd recently been through similar experiences allowed me to visualize concrete paths to my plans. When I ventured into a new opportunity, I felt a step ahead because I had her knowledge to fall back on. It's almost four years later and she's still a dear friend and a trusted advisor of mine.

My understanding of mentors has changed over the years. I used to think I had none. Without realizing it, I dismissed all the ways people touched my life and brought me where I am today. Mentors are everywhere. They're a trusted high school advisor who helps you navigate tough choices. They're a peer who you aspire to emulate. They're a friend, parent, or stranger who emboldens you to apply for that job or certification which propels you into your next phase of life. These seemingly small instances add up people, and can be greatly impactful. You never know when a few words of encouragement or a humble piece of advice is exactly what someone else needs to hear.

In thinking about all the ways I had been mentored by others, it dawned on me that I, too, regularly offer words of guidance to the people in my life. I never *really* considered myself a mentor. "Mentor" feels like such a weighty word, a role that equates to significant experience and expertise. I don't always feel far enough in my career to hold this title. Somewhere along the way, I found myself mentoring others as part of a daily practice and observing the benefits of this valuable relationship.

In my current role, I manage a program for teenagers and young adults with cognitive disabilities. We offer social events throughout the greater Saint Louis community where we help our participants build the confidence to take risks and coach them as they learn from challenges. While running this program includes a little of everything, a core focus of my role is to understand and teach others the intricacies involved in creating meaningful relationships. Connecting with others isn't always easy. What comes naturally to many doesn't come naturally to all. We start with some basics: how to pick up on social cues, what are the boundaries between a stranger, acquaintance, and friend, or understanding how to start and stop conversations. The basics are instrumental in learning how to identify the small moments with other people that tell us about our relationships with them. In the process of breaking down the foundations of relationships to other people, I realized I could benefit from this process myself.

As a Senior LeadHERship Fellow, in a small survey of close to one hundred people between the ages of eighteen to twenty-six years old, we asked people to answer the question: "What is a mentor?" We found that most definitions used guiding, advising, teaching, and coaching to describe mentors. These were the same verbs I used to describe all sorts of relationships in my personal and professional life. I thought back to the different clubs and organizations I was a mentor in but called my role by a different name. When volunteering with elementary school children, I was tutoring students, certainly not mentoring them. In my current role, I was coaching participants, totally different from mentoring someone. I was caught up in the semantics. "Mentor" is merely a synonym for advisor, teacher, or coach. At the core of all these roles, is sharing relevant knowledge from one person to the next.

Upon reflection, I learned not to overthink the relationship between mentor and mentee. Mentorship truly can be as simple as passing knowledge and skills from one person or the next generation. It was easy to move through life without realizing the role I played as a mentor, advisor, or teacher. In getting caught up in small details, it was easy to miss the bigger picture: the impact we make on others.

We often talk about the benefits of mentorship as increasing your network or taking you one step closer to securing a job opportunity. While those are both key benefits of mentorship, there are many other areas of growth that aren't as commonly highlighted for mentors and mentees.

Mentoring offers a comprehensive view of your industry as you engage with new or different perspectives that take you outside the bounds of your immediate role. Sometimes, these perspectives span across generations which brings whole swaths of new ideas into an industry. When relaying information to others, you in turn develop a better understanding of the concepts or material. You'll likely strengthen your leadership qualities and receive a confidence boost. It's flattering when others want to learn from you, and signals that you've got knowledge to share that others find important. My personal favorite benefit of being a mentor is that you have a hand in molding the future leaders in your industry. The wisdom or guidance you share will go on to shape the careers of those new to the industry, letting your legacy radiate through the people you guide and mentor.

For the mentees, the opportunity to engage with mentors also brings various benefits. You gain access to the perspective of someone who may have gone through similar experiences and can give you key advice to help you navigate the industry landscape. You'll have a chance for feedback about your goals or plans for the future, which in turn improves your communication skills. Communicating your ideas in a professional manner and in a way that is easily digestible is important for thriving in and out of the workplace. You will likely get the chance to witness someone from a similar background excel in your field. This alone can be great fuel to continue on with your career journey as it makes your own goals feel that much more achievable. Having this representation is especially important for people of marginalized or minority backgrounds who may not have access to these opportunities as often as non-marginalized or non-minority groups.

For both the mentor and the mentee, the relationship between the two offers a chance to shift away from an individualistic mindset. We move through life frequently centering ourselves and personal agendas. In a rush, it is easy to forget that it's beneficial to consider other perspectives. For mentorship to be successful, you must focus, listen, and learn from the other person. This relationship offers a chance to step out of an individualistic mindset and strengthen your ties to those around you. In doing so, you'll play a role in sustaining the communities to which you belong.

All these benefits can be observed from a simple conversation with another. What's discussed in any given conversation may not feel particularly life-changing or radical. The two small moments I shared with my advisor and friend weren't groundbreaking conversations that occurred. I'm positive neither my advisor nor friend even remember these moments. Still, those moments of mentorship greatly shaped my journey.

Mentorship, as I've come to understand it, is uniquely intertwined with our communities. Who we become is a mere reflection of where we've been and the people who have touched our lives. I am a reflection of the countless people who've offered me wisdom or guidance, my friends who approach me with love, and family members who exercise compassion. The ways we interact with people both big and small are impactful. Our words matter. Our thoughts matter. Our actions matter. For better or worse, each day we move through the world shaping each other. Aim to leave a legacy that is worthwhile.

Kate Wilkins is currently working as the Young Adult Program Manager at Pathways to Independence. Her day-to-day includes event planning and coordination, curriculum development, and strategic development for program growth. She studied at Washington University in Saint Louis where she graduated with honors and received a BA in International Studies, a BS in Psychology and Brain Sciences, and a minor in Legal Studies. As a military child, she is a six-time Folds of Honor recipient and four-time Hero's Legacy recipient.

She is passionate about working with underserved populations and has previously worked with students in inner-city schools in Saint Louis, spoke as a peer educator for Leaders in Interpersonal Violence Education, and worked at Washington University's Disability Resource Center. In her personal life, she currently enjoys baking, water coloring, yoga, and going for walks through many of Saint Louis County's parks.

Please scan the QR code to connect with this author.

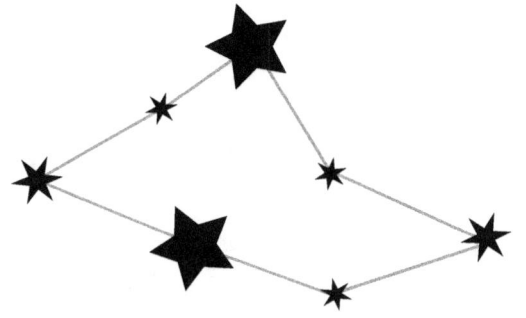

LeadHERship
Fellows Stars

The LeadHERship Mission

Sponsored by: Rachel Rubin Wilkins
Founder of Team of Seven, LLC
TW Legacy Publishing

The 2024–2025 LeadHERship Fellows program was created to support the need for additional leadership, career guidance, and mentorship to support college students and young professionals. After a successful Team of Seven Summer Internship, fellows were chosen to continue and receive an advanced opportunity to learn about event management in the profit and non-profit areas, enhance skills associated with event marketing and management, and basic fundraising goals through local non-profits. In addition, this year the fellows had the unique opportunity to be a part of the process of professional publishing. Each fellow chose how they wanted to contribute to The Lead, Lift, and Leave a Legacy anthology. They received the Recognize the Stars in Your Constellations Workshop, coaching and mentoring, networking opportunities, tours of local businesses, and career development.

Here are the 2024–2025 LeadHERship Fellows and their contributions to the Lead, Lift, and Leave a Legacy Collection of remarkable women:

Remi Barnett—research assistant, marketing, social media, mentoring survey, endorsements

Audrey Pinson—marketing, social media, co-authoring, mentoring survey contributor

Hanah Wilkins—research assistant and co-author, marketing, social media, mentoring survey

Sarah Wilkins—chapter co-author, marketing, social media, mentoring survey contributor

Senior LeadHERship Fellow:

Kate Wilkins—chapter co-author, marketing, social media, mentoring survey editor

Thank you, ladies, for your time and dedication to this mission and your contribution to the evolution of what LeadHERship and mentoring mean for our next generation of leaders. My goals for you during this fellowship were to give you tangible skills that facilitate self-efficacy, reflection, and gratitude, knowing that there are remarkable women within reach to network with and enhance your personal and professional lives, while being a positive light for others to see and emulate, believing in the power of relationships. The ripple effect of these relationships is all around you!

I am grateful for you and wish you the best as you wrap up your college career and soar into the future as shooting stars! You can count on me to be a mentor, coach, advisor, or sponsor along your journey!

Keep Shining—
Rachel (Mom, Mrs. Wilkins)

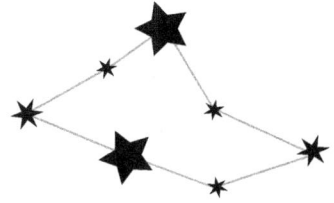

Sarah A. Wilkins

Silent Threads

I hold a special place in my heart for all service members and their families. As the youngest of five children born into a military family, my upbringing does not reflect the typical childhood most Americans are familiar with. My dad retired from the Army when I started sixth grade, which introduced me to the American civilian lifestyle. After having a foot in both worlds for some time, there is one woman who comes to mind when I consider what it means to be a silent mentor and contributor to your community, and to whom I can relate through both footholds: Roslyn Schulte.

During my time as an Army brat, I moved to six different states and two countries before the age of thirteen. Along the way, my dad deployed ten times between Afghanistan and Iraq. From Washington to Kansas, Georgia, Virginia, Italy, and Missouri, my mom had been a constant force of stability, leading us through each transition with so much grace. From what I remember, the continuous overturn from place to place was natural, and I commend my mom so much for creating a sense of normalcy each time. Within my five brothers and sisters, my mom cultivated an air of resilience and steadfast assurance in our abilities to overcome hardships. Even though we grew up in changing environments, she never failed to make us feel seen, heard, or have a place to call home.

In sixth grade, we made our final move to St. Louis where our family retired after 20 years of active-duty service. At first, I found my new community unfamiliar and somewhat uninviting; it was hard to build friendships with kids who had known everybody around them from a young age, and I was severely unaccustomed to being one of the only new kids on the block. It took some time, but we all managed the adjustment period and in our own time found our places among the crowd. Being properly acclimated to the part of society where kids spend their childhood in one house, in one neighborhood with deep-rooted connections to family and friends around them, I recognize the strength needed to exist and succeed as a military family. In St. Louis, I spent a year attending public school before transitioning to attend John Burroughs School. Upon acceptance into the school, I was awarded the *Roslyn L. Schulte Memorial Scholarship*.

Roslyn, the woman this scholarship honors, was a Burroughs graduate and St. Louis native. After attending the Air Force Academy, Roslyn lost her life to a roadside bomb in Afghanistan; she was 25 at the time of her death. Roslyn was the first woman awarded the National Intelligence Medal for Valor. She was also awarded the Bronze Star and Purple Heart, among many other accolades. I look back and realize how much I have grown to understand the sacrifices people make, and the legacy these contributions have on their communities. Roslyn was someone who carried herself with grace and poise, steadfast engagement, and a fierce competitive edge. In seventh grade, I had so much to learn about her besides the honor of her scholarship. It is one thing to receive a scholarship awarded in someone's name and memory. It is another to truly understand who this scholarship is memorializing and what the cost of their loss is within their family, community, and life potential. I was immensely appreciative of the opportunities her scholarship gave me, for

I felt its contributions to my life throughout my time at Burroughs. For a time, I felt disconnected from Roslyn's story because she was, in a sense, a stranger to me.

As I've grown older, there are little moments that draw me back to Roslyn's story, which I have been piecing together for years to understand exactly why I resonate with her so much. Over time, these moments of connection come together to show me some of the threads forming her life's tapestry. I have an undying fondness for the tenacity and light exuded from her friends' and family's recollections of her, and the impact she has left behind through her numerous accomplishments. Although in some ways Roslyn will always remain unfamiliar to me, I have grown to see her as a silent mentor through the legacy she has left among her friends, family, and communities.

Unlike me, Roslyn grew up in St. Louis. I used to wonder what exactly it was that drew her to want to serve as a member of the military when she grew up in an environment, I found to be so separate from the military sphere. She was the type of person to see the importance of fighting for something larger than herself, placing other people's safety over her own, time and time again. To see that quality in Roslyn, that willingness to give so much, is breathtaking. I imagine this core virtue showed through in so many of her endeavors, one being her contributions to her lacrosse teams. Roslyn was a captain of both her high school and college lacrosse teams, and her family is a huge reason lacrosse is now such an established sport at Burroughs. Being a leader, or mentor, means you have certain qualities that draw people into you and push people to look up to you. On the lacrosse field, she was spirited, encouraging, and a determined contender to play against. While captaining her high school team, they won a state championship. In addition, she was recognized as an All-American athlete in lacrosse. I do not underestimate how her leadership contributed to these accomplishments. Additionally, I catch myself smiling about the fact that she continued to lead in this realm during her college years, honing her skills in leadership positions and dominating on the field, just as she did in her high school years. Roslyn's accomplishments exemplify so many of the characteristics I look up to in a mentor. Unexpectedly, Roslyn's legacy would thread heavily through my own high school and college experiences.

During my senior year of high school, our field hockey field was named the Lt. Roslyn Schulte 02' Field in her honor. Our school held an assembly to commemorate the new field and its memorialization of Roslyn. Prior to this assembly, I did not know the extent to which I would see our similarities and understand how pivotal her legacy would be to my understanding of myself. Thankfully, with time comes development, and now my knowledge, admiration, and commitment to her legacy have largely influenced who I am today. During the assembly announcement, some of her former classmates took it upon themselves to share some memories of her with the student body, so we could all get to know her a little better. My field hockey and lacrosse coach, Janie, was close friends with her and talked so highly of the times they spent together in high school and the years after. As Janie shared, pictures of Roslyn were presented on the screen hanging behind her. I could follow Janie's words, seeing them come to life through the enthusiasm Roslyn exuded, her personality becoming so much clearer. I remember sitting in my assembly seat feeling incredibly moved when a particular image emerged on the screen.

Roslyn stood, frozen in the moment, with her hands on her hips. She was smiling, sporting a bright blue wig, yellow feather boa, and the jersey number 21. Looking up, I was dumbfounded, and I felt chills. Since my freshman year of high school, I have been drawn to wear the number 21 in competition. I wore it all of my high school years and as captain my junior year. Before this assembly, I had no idea we shared that connection. At WashU, I still wear the same number on my college club lacrosse team. Since that assembly, every time I have put my jersey on, I think about wearing it for her.

As a captain at WashU, it warms me to think we shared similar commitments in high school and college. Since that moment in the assembly hall, my understanding of the purpose of my reception of Roslyn's scholarship changed thoroughly. I will always feel her presence in a way that is closely tied to my life, in our commitments to competition, but also in the way I show up for my community. For me, Roslyn is a powerful example of the ways I can contribute to my community, on and off the field.

Another moment that solidifies my connection to Roslyn's story happened while visiting the Flags of Valor on Art Hill in St. Louis, a yearly tradition my family embarks on. These flags are placed every year on the hill to commemorate the lives lost in combat since September 11th. Every year the view from across the Forest Park Basin is striking. The hill has rows of flags filling the spaces where you would normally find people basking in the grass. Our first time attending, out of the hundreds of flags waving on the hill against the backdrop of the art museum, my mom and I walked up to one and turned the dog tags over to read them. That first flag was Roslyn's, with a picture of her in uniform and her dog tags hanging from the pole, clattering against the metal in tune with the wind. This experience, similar to that feeling of intense connection I felt during that assembly, was astounding. Out of the 7,000 other tags there, we touched hers first. I feel there is nothing besides divine intention that led us to her flag first, an intentional message from the universe that Roslyn's memory will always be something to hold close to me.

Ultimately, Roslyn is a woman I look to for strength, courage, guidance, and empowerment. Through her, I have learned that awareness of the legacy you can leave behind is vital. You may not understand how intensely you can affect those you know or the strangers who see your legacy and resonate with it. Roslyn, for me, will always be a mentor. She is someone who I want to live my best life for, to give my all in any condition I am placed in. She excelled at field hockey and lacrosse, and every time I step onto the field I try to play like her, for her. I want to make her proud. Additionally, Roslyn's zeal to engage academically with her subjects, and the compassion and commitment she had to connect with her peers, is something I turn back to when I feel myself dragging. Her ability to so deftly understand what she wanted her life trajectory to be, the way she was able to accomplish so much, to push herself in all directions along the way, models the self-reliance and integrity I find myself wanting to lean towards in my own life path.

I know that as the years go on, who she was will be there to guide me. Roslyn has helped me understand who I want to become. She has empowered me. While I will never have the privilege to meet her, I can feel her legacy reflected in my coach and mentor, Janie, in Roslyn's family's recollections of her, in my relationship with my childhood as an Army brat, and in the transitions I have faced and will continue to face with the movement of my life.

Sarah Wilkins is a young woman from St. Louis, Missouri. She attended high school at John Burroughs School, graduating with honors. She participated and was a captain of her field hockey team, cheerleading squad, and lacrosse teams. She now attends Washington University in St. Louis in the class of 2026. Sarah is an English Literature Major and Spanish minor. At WashU, she has been a captain and executive chair member of the Women's Club Lacrosse team since the Spring of her freshman year. She has made the Dean's List twice and is a recurring Folds of Honor recipient. In 2024 she was a part of the Team of Seven's Summer Intern program and is currently participating in the 2024/25 LeadHERship Fellows Program. By obtaining her yoga teacher certification before returning to graduate school for her PhD in English literature, Sarah aspires to facilitate safe spaces for these communities to engage with their interests.

Please scan the QR code to connect with this author.

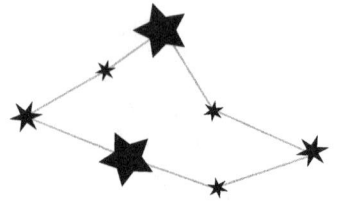

Audrey Pinson

It Starts with You

Being your own mentor is about cultivating a foundation so solid that you no longer feel the need to stand alone. It's about striking a balance between drawing valuable insight from within yourself and staying open to the lessons others bring into your life. Growing up, I never truly grasped the consequences of death and the long-term impact it fosters. Attending countless funerals as a child and losing loved ones at a young age, the longevity of loss and emotional turmoil hadn't struck me deeper than being sad for a couple of days, missing someone I didn't truly know, and moving on. It wasn't until my Grandpa passed away in 2022 that I found myself standing face-to-face with a new reality. A reality where death lingers and holds power over your life in ways you hadn't felt before. Experiencing loss as an adult felt more extreme than any other experiences I've had in the past. The finality of my Grandpa's passing was a stark wake-up call. This first encounter with death as an adult made me realize how fleeting moments truly are, and that I had been prioritizing the wrong things in life. It dawned on me that I was growing up.

As a nineteen-year-old, just starting to gain a deeper consciousness about life, one that extended beyond myself, I didn't know how to navigate my emotions or manage the grief I felt for my mother, my family, and myself. It left me feeling paralyzed, unable to truly help or comfort anyone. I realized I was stuck in a cycle of obsessing over things that no longer served me. I wanted to show up for my family, but I knew I couldn't pour from an empty cup. I needed to face the unresolved parts of myself first. It's here that I found my purpose; not only in healing but in sharing the journey with others. I want women to find comfort in knowing they're not alone when life feels overwhelming. I want to show that pain and loss don't have to define us. We can transform hardships into empowerment and build stepping stones toward self-mentorship and leadership. Healing is not a solitary act but a deliberate decision to help ourselves so we can eventually open the door for others to help us too. This chapter is a testament to that belief: through grief, reflection, and a commitment to growth, we can find strength in ourselves to lead and lift others with our shared experiences.

I remember sitting in the communal kitchen of my freshman dorm with the lights off and the sink water running, to ensure no one could overhear my conversation. I hesitated as I dialed the number on my phone, feeling ashamed and embarrassed. It was so difficult for me to accept that I needed some guidance, but I knew no one could help me unless I helped myself first. I held back tears as I spoke with the mental health provider on the phone and scheduled my first therapy appointment. She told me it took courage to reach out for help. She was proud of me. She didn't understand how much I needed to hear that. Something about this moment confirmed that I was headed in a direction that would forever change my trajectory. I realized that *my healing journey starts with me.*

Through therapy, I began breaking free from the victim mentality that had consumed me. For so long, I viewed life as something happening to me. I believed people were deliberately causing me harm, the universe was stripping things away from me, and I was powerless in the face of these circumstances. My mindset had become deeply cynical, but I began to realize that the key to escaping this narrative lay within myself. The first step was taking accountability; not only for my choices, but also for the perspective I had chosen to adopt. Pulling myself out of a perspective I'd become so comfortable with was unbelievably challenging. I felt as if I was anchored in a sea of cynicism and disillusionment, bound by relationships that felt shallow and transactional. I started to see how I had played a role in my own circumstances. I was allowing others to treat me poorly, holding on to connections I knew lacked sincerity, and consciously maintaining an obsessive fixation on the past. I found myself trapped in an endless loop of retrospection, dissecting memories in search of closure that never materialized. I began to understand the way I interpreted my circumstances. It was the lens through which I viewed the world. This is when I was introduced to the concept of emotional autonomy; the idea that I had the power to control my outlook and, by extension, my emotional experience.

This realization was both liberating and daunting. Knowing that I held the ability to shape how I felt about situations was exhilarating, yet it came with the weight of responsibility. I understood that nothing in life is inherently good or bad; the emotions we attach to events are what define them. However, by shifting my perspective, I could find silver linings in moments of loss and growth in the challenges I once deemed insurmountable. What I once viewed as 'bad things happening to me' became opportunities to learn, adapt, and evolve. It's difficult to separate the concept of therapy and my personal therapist when speaking generally, however, I believe my therapist became more than just a professional resource. She became a mentor. Unlike traditional mentors who might focus on specific skills or goals, a therapist's mentorship is deeply personal and introspective. She didn't simply tell me what to do or how to feel; she asked the questions I hadn't thought to ask myself. She encouraged me to examine my beliefs. What made her mentorship so impactful was that it wasn't about solving my problems for me; it was about equipping me with the tools to solve them on my own. She helped me understand that emotional autonomy wasn't just about controlling my feelings but about recognizing that I had a choice in how I responded to life's challenges. Through this, I came to see mentorship in a broader light. My therapist's guidance opened my eyes to the ways other people in my life had mentored me without me realizing it.

These shifts in perspective did not happen overnight. My nights as a college student were atypical. I stayed in my dorm room, journaled for hours on end, listened to podcasts, called my parents, and reflected on my choices and actions that had led me to this point. It was isolating and I felt extremely lonely for months. However, it was in these moments, confined to the seclusion of my room, where solitude began to transform from a source of loneliness into a space for self-discovery. The lessons I learned about transforming feelings of loss into opportunities for growth naturally led me to cultivate a profound sense of gratitude for the things I do have in life. I began to appreciate my solidified friendships, my supportive family, my cat, and even the simple yet extraordinary privilege of being able to move my body.

Gratitude became a cornerstone of my daily life, a way to remind myself of what truly matters, especially during moments of darkness when joy can feel elusive. This realization deepened my commitment to being present, as I came to see how closely gratitude and presence are intertwined. I started to act on this value intentionally, finding ways to anchor myself in the present while expressing my gratitude. It was through this practice of gratitude, and the mindset shifts guided by my therapist, that I began to truly see my mom as the mentor she has always been. For so long, I had taken her unwavering support, her sacrifices, and her wisdom for granted, viewing them as constants in my life without recognizing the depth of her influence. Gratitude transformed my relationship with her. Over the last few years, as I worked to heal and practice thankfulness, our bond deepened in ways I couldn't have imagined. By acknowledging and appreciating everything she does for me, not just in big or noticeable ways but also in the quiet moments, I've come to understand the full impact of her presence in my life. I've learned that when you approach relationships with gratitude, you create space for them to flourish. And in doing this work, I've realized that *it all starts within.*

A mantra that guided me through this process was, 'Energy goes where your attention flows.' This phrase grounded me during moments when I was tempted to slip back into cynicism or ruminate on the past. It served as a reminder that my focus shapes my reality, and by redirecting my attention to the present and all it had to offer, I could craft a life filled with purpose. Ultimately, I came to understand that perspective is everything. It defines your truth and becomes your reality.

Transitioning into my early 20s, I've expanded on a lot of these lessons learned from earlier in my college career and I believe that I wouldn't be the same person without them. College is often portrayed as a time of boundless possibility and excitement, but for many, it is equally overwhelming and disorienting. Navigating the transition into adulthood brings its own unique challenges, and this universal experience inevitably impacted my mental health. I learned, however, that adaptability and flexibility are crucial skills during this stage of life, particularly when things don't unfold as planned. I've come to firmly believe that everything happens for a reason, even if the path I'm on doesn't immediately make sense. Its purpose will become clear in time. Adopting this mindset has allowed me to put common stressors, such as career decisions and grades, into perspective. I no longer view them as monumental, but rather as steps in an ever-evolving journey.

Not having a rigid plan is part of the beauty of being in your 20s. There's an immense pressure on people my age to have everything figured out: a career trajectory, a five-year plan, a clear sense of direction. I've come to see the value in embracing uncertainty. While it's important to move toward goals and put yourself out there, this decade should be a time for experimentation, failure, and recalibration. I've struggled with career anxiety. It's something I continue to work through, but I've started to question the notion of success. Does success inherently mean impressing others? I don't believe so. To me, success is deeply personal and can take on countless forms, depending on one's values and aspirations. It's about aligning with my authentic self, learning from missteps, and creating a life defined not by external validation but by fulfillment and growth.

In these earlier years of adulthood, I came to understand that the power I have over my life is the most important. The concept of mentorship is often highlighted as an essential element for growth. While I recognize the value of having a mentor, I can't say I've ever had one in the traditional sense. I've had people in my life who supported me and offered guidance, but when I reflect on my journey, I realize that I've largely been my own mentor through the most challenging moments. This self-reliance has fostered a deep trust and comfort within me, allowing me to develop emotional intelligence at a younger age. What does it really mean to be your own mentor? For me, it's about cultivating the ability to navigate difficult emotions, make decisions with intention, and guide myself through uncertainty. It's about recognizing my own strength, learning from my experiences, embracing change, and trusting my intuition. It has taught me that I am capable of leading myself with compassion and clarity, even in the absence of external direction.

Being your own mentor isn't just about independence; it's about getting to a place where you don't *need* to be. True self-mentorship means creating the emotional foundation that allows you to feel secure enough to accept help from others, to trust their support without losing your sense of self. It's about being strong enough to stand on your own but open enough to recognize the ways others influence your life, your perspective, and your growth. Yes, it starts with you, but it doesn't end there. In fact, this openness is what makes mentorship in all its forms so transformative. When you've done the work to guide yourself, you can better appreciate the guidance and wisdom that others provide. You become more attuned to the value of their presence and the lessons they bring into your life. For me, this realization has deepened my relationships and taught me that true strength lies in striking balance. It's about being your own source of wisdom while still welcoming the influence of those who inspire, uplift, and lead you to be better. Perhaps from this, we can be that person for others.

Audrey Pinson is a photojournalism major at the University of Missouri – Columbia with a minor in Fine Art. She currently works as an intern for MyrtleHaus Magazine, an art-focused and woman-led publication that features local artists in the St. Louis area. She also works as a photojournalist and content creator for Turning Point, a homeless shelter in Columbia, that aims to destigmatize the concept of homelessness and depicts clients in an accurate light. She has a deep passion for storytelling and visual art which has guided her to take advantage of these kinds of opportunities. Over the last year, she has had the honor of working with Team of Seven and being a part of the LeadHERship fellows. Connecting with other women, hearing their stories, and gaining new perspectives on mentorship has been extremely impactful for her. In her free time, she loves hiking, singing and playing guitar, and journaling!

Please scan the QR code to connect with this author.

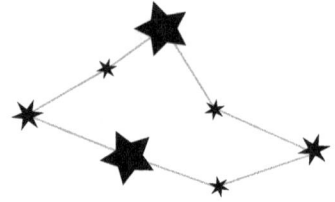

Hanah Wilkins

Mentoring: A Younger Generation's Perspective

Having a mentor is a great way to gain experience in a field and form new relationships, both professionally and personally. Traditionally, a mentor is experienced with a specific field and can offer advice, guidance, and support to their mentee, who is either interested in or currently working in that field. With the rise of technology, it has changed how professional and personal relationships are made by increasing the exposure to people with more diverse backgrounds and experiences. While this allows for a wider range of mentors, it can also prevent more personal relationships from forming if there is no in-person contact. In this way, it is important to understand the perspective of mentoring from the younger generations, who grew up in this new age.

Demographics

To find how young adults both in and out of college perceive mentorship, the LeadHERship Fellows created a survey to send out to their peers, receiving 88 responses by the beginning of January. The ages of participants ranged from 18 to 30 years old, with the most common ages being 20 (35.2%), 21 (29.5%) and 25 (10.2%) years old. Of these, 77% identified as female, 23% identified as male, and 0% identified as non-binary or preferred not to answer. Regarding race and ethnicity of the respondents, 74.7% were white, 16.6% were Hispanic or Latino, 12.7% were Black or African American, 7.6% were Asian, and 2.5% were Native American. The majority of the respondents were in college (84.1%), while the other 15.9% were employed, transitioning schools, enrolled in certification classes, or pursuing an advanced degree. Here is the chart of the universities the respondents attend:

What college/university do you currently attend?
74 responses

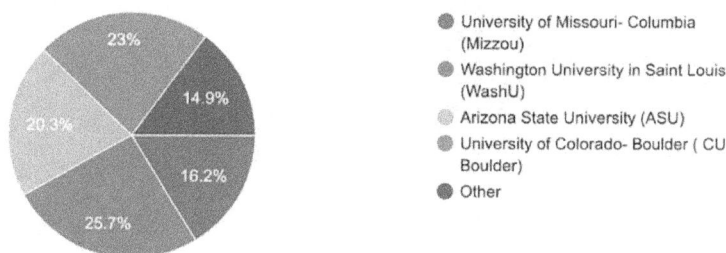

Over 92 different degrees are being pursued, a few being: Behavioral Sciences, Statistics, Business, Journalism, PreMed, Anthropology, International Studies, Nursing, Chemistry, Mechanical Engineering, Integrated Physiology, Computer science, Sociology, and Film.

Networking

When asked to define networking, there were a variety of responses relating to communication and professional relationships. The most common ideas mentioned in the free responses included meeting people, building relationships, and connecting with other people who have similar interests. The participants were then asked how many networking or social events they attended each month, and the majority (47.1%) said zero, while 41.4% of respondents attended one to three events per month.

Almost all respondents agreed (95.5%) that networking would enhance their social capital when asked. Similarly, 73.9% of the participants said yes when asked whether they thought networking is important in finding a mentor or enhancing their career journey, while 22.7% said maybe. Here is the chart for that question:

Do you think networking is important in finding a mentor or enhancing your career journey?
88 responses

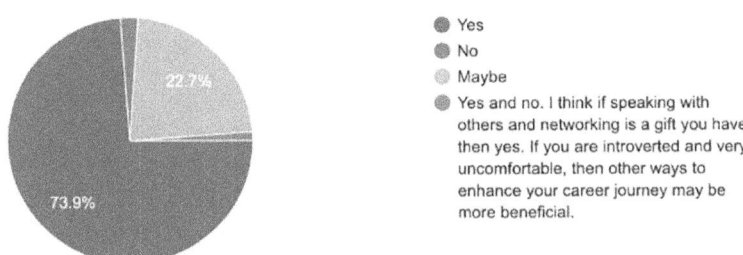

Yes
No
Maybe
Yes and no. I think if speaking with others and networking is a gift you have, then yes. If you are introverted and very uncomfortable, then other ways to enhance your career journey may be more beneficial.

Mentoring

A mentor is defined by Merriam-Webster as a trusted counselor or guide. This definition is reflected in the answers from the respondents of this survey. When asked the question "What is a mentor" the respondent provided an array of answers, the most common word used to answer the question being "guide", which was in 42.3% of answers, while "advice" was in 28%, and "experience" was in 14.1%. 70.5% of the participants believed that mentors were not needed to gain opportunities or advance their careers, although they are nice to have, while 28.4% said they are needed. When asked what qualities they would look for in a mentor, "experienced" and "knowledgeable" were used most often (31.5%), "kind" was mentioned in 19.7% of answers, and "honesty" and "understanding" were mentioned in 14.5% of answers. Even though the participants knew what characteristics they wanted in a mentor, only 55.7% of the respondents knew where to find a mentor, while 44.5% did not. Of the respondents

47.1% had one to two mentors, 20.7% had no mentors, 17.2% had four or more mentors, and 14.9% had three to four mentors. These mentors included *senior mentors, silent mentors,* and *peer mentors.* We defined *senior mentors* as someone with career knowledge and experience in an industry, *silent mentors* as people you admire yet have not met, and *peer mentors* as people within five years of their age. When the participants were asked how they would use their mentor, the top three most common answers centered around learning about a job field and networking. 96% said they would ask their mentors for advice on experiences in the field, 92% said they would use them to connect with other professionals in relevant fields, and 89.6% said they would use them to hear about what works and what doesn't work in their field. Finally, 54% of the respondents believed that their professional relationships and resources were best found through a thoughtful combination of technology and personal relationships, while 41.4% thought only personal and professional relationships were best. Here is the chart for this question:

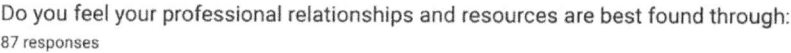

Do you feel your professional relationships and resources are best found through:
87 responses

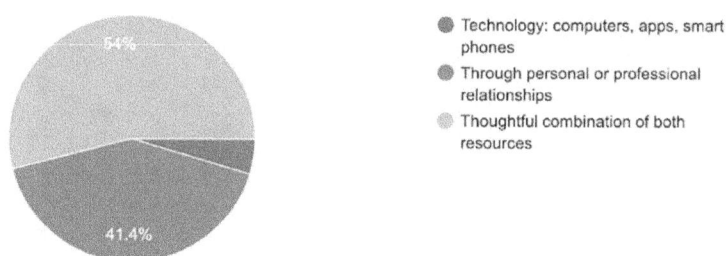

● Technology: computers, apps, smart phones
● Through personal or professional relationships
● Thoughtful combination of both resources

Conclusion

This survey showed us how mentorship is considered to be a valuable tool among young adults looking to start their networking and professional growth journey. The results highlight how young adults expressed a clear preference for characteristics in their mentors such as guidance, experience, and advice. The survey emphasizes how mentorship can facilitate gaining insights into a specific field, as well as networking, both of which young adults find important. Additionally, with the inclusion of technology, it shows how they navigate the world placing importance on balancing both in-person and online professional relationships. These findings underscore the importance of mentorship in shaping successful career paths while young adults begin to enter the professional world.

Hanah Wilkins is from St. Louis, Missouri where she graduated from John Burroughs High School. She is currently a junior studying Neuroscience and Psychology with a pre-health designation at the University of Colorado Boulder. She is a Folds of Honor Scholar, as well as a Heroes Legacy scholar, and was on the Dean's list in the spring of 2023 and fall of 2024. Hanah is also working as a LeadHERship fellow and previously worked as a Team of Seven intern. After graduating from college, she hopes to take a few years working in a research lab before applying to PA school. During the school year, Hanah works at the CU bookstore on-campus, and enjoys snowboarding, crocheting, listening to music, hiking, and hanging out with friends.

Please scan the QR code to connect with this author.

RESOURCE LISTINGS

teamofseven.com

Our TEAM is ready to assist you in developing and deploying a tailored strategic roadmap that drives your business to success at your next adventure!

TEAM- Together, Everyone Accomplishes More!

MovereCoaching.com

We empower leaders, professionals, and teams to unlock their strengths, lead authentically, and create thriving workplaces through coaching, leader development, and team effectiveness solutions.

Empowering Talent. Maximizing Strengths. Creating Momentum.

---

https://srvhr.com/tina-linnenbrink

We elevate HR for small, growth-minded businesses, guiding talent strategies, implementing scalable systems, and providing actionable, results-driven solutions that help businesses thrive.

HR Made **Simple**.

Build talent, scale smarter, thrive faster.

RESOURCE LISTINGS

Wildflowers STL

For unique, seasonally sourced floral arrangements, celebrating the beauty of nature for all of life's moments.

Artistic florals for all of life's moments.

---

marthashands.com

For 27 years, families have chosen Martha's Hands Home Care Services to assist their loved ones with their daily activities and support. We deliver care based on our mission of Love through Service.

Marianne Biangardi

"I am committed to leaving a lasting impact through kindness, service, and mentorship—values my mom instilled in me. Grateful for her legacy, I strive to uplift others, create meaningful connections, and inspire the next generation through generosity, gratitude, and mentorship."

RESOURCE LISTINGS

empoweredhomes.com

We help families meet their real estate needs by providing seamless transitions that bring peace of mind and lasting comfort for every generation.

EMPOWERED HOMES

Delivering the Joy of Home.

FierceCreative.agency

We are visual communicators building consistent and cohesive brand stories for those seeking more leads, sales or brand awareness through exceptional creative and growth strategies.

FIERCE
CREATIVE.AGENCY

Exceptional Creative. Cohesive Branding. Measurable Results.

---

paceproperties.com + www.avisonyoungstl.com

Pace Properties and Avison Young deliver expert commercial real estate solutions, leveraging deep market knowledge, strong relationships, and a collaborative approach to maximize client success.

PACE PROPERTIES
— SINCE 1984 —

AVISON YOUNG

Creating Value Through Experience

RESOURCE LISTINGS

TraversTraining.com

We offer dynamic speaking engagements, vital leadership development training, and focused HR business consulting, equipping your team for excellence. Our mission is to transform organizations and empower individuals.

TRAVERS

TRAINING & CONSULTING

Helping You Empower your People behind your Processes

LimitlessHorizonsConsulting.com

We provide nonprofits and philanthropic organizations with tailored services that amplify their mission and create lasting impact.

LH

CONSULTING

Accomplishing Your Mission

Southside-ecc.org

We create equitable, inclusive learning opportunities and support services for all children and families through education, health, connection, and thought leadership.

SouthSide
Early Childhood Center